THE 100+ SERIES™
READING COMPREHENSION

Essential Practice for Advanced Reading Comprehension Topics

Grade 1

Carson-Dellosa Publishing, LLC
Greensboro, North Carolina

Credits

Content Editor: Angela Triplett
Proofreader: Karen Seberg

Visit *carsondellosa.com* for correlations to Common Core, state, national, and Canadian provincial standards.

Carson-Dellosa Publishing, LLC
PO Box 35665
Greensboro, NC 27425 USA
carsondellosa.com

© 2015, Carson-Dellosa Publishing, LLC. The purchase of this material entitles the buyer to reproduce worksheets and activities for classroom use only—not for commercial resale. Reproduction of these materials for an entire school or district is prohibited. No part of this book may be reproduced (except as noted above), stored in a retrieval system, or transmitted in any form or by any means (mechanically, electronically, recording, etc.) without the prior written consent of Carson-Dellosa Publishing, LLC.

Printed in the USA • All rights reserved.

ISBN 978-1-4838-1559-6
02-235167784

Table of Contents

Table of Contents/Introduction 3	Fact or Opinion 83
Common Core Alignment Chart 4	Making Inferences 87
Sequencing 5	Story Elements: Character 92
Classifying 12	Story Elements: Setting 97
Main Idea 20	Story Elements: Plot 102
Identifying Details 26	Story Elements: Mixed 105
Summarizing 38	Following Directions 109
Context Clues 43	Cloze 112
Compare and Contrast 50	Generalizing 116
Cause and Effect 61	Charts and Graphs 118
Making Predictions 69	Answer Key 123
Reality or Fantasy 77	

Introduction

Organized by specific reading skills, this book is designed to enhance students' reading comprehension. The engaging topics provide meaningful and focused practice. The reading passages are presented in a variety of genres, including fiction, nonfiction, and poetry. Subject matter from across the curriculum, including topics from science, history, and literary classics, deepens student knowledge while strengthening reading skills.

The grade-appropriate selections in this series are an asset to any reading program. Various reading skills and concepts are reinforced throughout the book through activities that align to the Common Core State Standards in English language arts. To view these standards, please see the Common Core Alignment Chart on page 4.

Common Core Alignment Chart

Common Core State Standards*		Practice Page(s)
Reading Standards for Literature		
Key Ideas and Details	1.RL.1–1.RL.3	8, 10, 12–15, 17–19, 23, 26, 27, 30–33, 35, 36, 38, 42, 48, 49, 60, 64, 71, 73, 76, 78–82, 84, 85, 88, 89, 91–97, 99–115
Craft and Structure	1.RL.4–1.RL.6	14, 20, 35, 42, 60, 85, 94, 95, 99–101, 106
Integration of Knowledge and Ideas	1.RL.7–1.RL.9	8, 10, 15, 17–20, 23, 27, 30–32, 38, 48, 49, 60, 64, 71, 73–75, 78, 80, 88, 89, 92, 96, 100–103, 109–111
Range of Reading and Level of Text Complexity	1.RL.10	8, 10, 12–15, 17–20, 23, 26, 27, 30–33, 35–38, 42, 60, 64, 71, 73–76, 78, 79, 82, 85, 92–97, 99–109, 112–115
Reading Standards for Informational Text		
Key Ideas and Details	1.RI.1–1.RI.3	5–7, 9, 11, 16, 21, 22, 24, 28, 29, 34, 39–41, 43–45, 50–59, 61–63, 65–70, 77, 83, 86, 87, 90, 98, 116–118
Craft and Structure	1.RI.4–1.RI.6	34, 43–46, 50, 51, 70, 72, 90, 118–122
Integration of Knowledge and Ideas	1.RI.7–1.RI.9	5–7, 9, 16, 28, 29, 43–46, 50–59, 61–63, 66–70, 72, 77, 87, 90, 98, 117
Range of Reading and Level of Text Complexity	1.RI.10	5–7, 9, 11, 16, 20–22, 24, 28, 29, 34, 39–41, 43–46, 50–59, 61–63, 65–70, 77, 83, 86, 87, 90, 98
Reading Standards: Foundational Skills		
Phonics and Word Recognition	1.RF.3	47
Fluency	1.RF.4	49
Writing Standards		
Text Types and Purposes	1.W.1–1.W.3	10, 11, 46, 48, 84, 88
Language Standards		
Vocabulary Acquisition and Use	1.L.4–1.L.6	47, 112–115

* © Copyright 2010. National Governors Association Center for Best Practices and Council of Chief State School Officers. All rights reserved.

Name_____

Sequencing

Read the story.

The Bus

The bus takes people many places.

First, the bus takes people to .

Next, it stops at a . Then, it goes

to the . The bus helps people all day long.

Circle the correct answer.

1. Where can you go on a bus?

   A.

   B.

   C.

3. Where does the bus go last?

   A.

   B.

   C.

2. Where does the bus go first?

   A.

   B.

   C.

4. What is the main idea of this story?

   _____
   _____
   _____
   _____
   _____

Name_____

Sequencing

Read the story.

Trains

Trains ride on tracks. The 🚂 pulls the train. Each 🚃 is part of the train. Sometimes, a train has a red 🚋 at the end.

Circle the correct answer.

1. What pulls the train?

    A.
    B.
    C.

2. What comes next on the train?

    A.
    B.
    C.

3. What is at the end of the train?

    A.
    B.
    C.

4. Trains ride on

    _____.

6
© Carson-Dellosa • CD-104839

Name_____

Sequencing

Read the story.

Ice Cream

Ice cream comes in many yummy flavors.

How do you make an ?

Dip a ⌒ of ice cream.

Put the ⌒ on the ▽.

Eat your !

Ice cream is good on a hot day.

Complete the activities.

1. Put the steps in order.
   Write **1**, **2**, or **3**.

   _____ Put the ⌒ on the ▽.

   _____ Eat your .

   _____ Dip a ⌒ of ice cream.

2. Ice cream is good on a
   _____.

3. Circle your favorite flavor.

   chocolate

   vanilla

   strawberry

4. What is the main idea of this story?

   _____

   _____

Name_____

Sequencing

Read the story.

The Baseball Game

Cody and his dad go to a baseball game. First, they sit down. Then, Cody eats a . His dad eats some . The game is good. Their team hits a home run! Cody and his dad have fun.

Circle the correct answer.

1. What does Cody and his dad do first?

    A. eat food

    B. hit a home run

    C. sit down

2. What does Cody eat?

    A.

    B.

    C.

3. What happens in the baseball game?

    A. Their team eats food.

    B. Their team has fun.

    C. Their team hits a home run.

4. Have you ever been to a baseball game?

    Yes   No

8

© Carson-Dellosa • CD-104839

Name_____

Sequencing

Read the story.

The Spider

A spider finds a good place for a home. She spins a web. She works hard. She waits for a fly. The fly will be her dinner.

Circle the correct answer.

1. What does the spider do first?

    A. finds a good place for a home

    B. waits for a fly

    C. works hard

2. What does the spider do last?

    A. spins a web

    B. waits for a fly

    C. works hard

3. What is a spider's home called?

    A. web

    B. net

    C. hive

4. What do spiders eat?

    A. toads

    B. flies

    C. snakes

Read the poem.

Penny

Penny is a pack rat.
She owns many things.
She has a hat, two baseball bats,
And three shiny rings.
Now, Penny wants a new toy van,
A mouse trap, and a little fan!

Circle the correct answer.

1. What does Penny own now?

    A. a new toy van

    B. a mouse trap

    C. two baseball bats

2. What does Penny want?

    A. a hat

    B. a little fan

    C. three shiny rings

3. How many things does Penny own now?

    A. two

    B. three

    C. six

4. What would you like to own? Write a sentence to tell why.

    _____
    _____
    _____
    _____

Name_____

Sequencing

Read the story.

Days

There are seven days in a week. Sunday is the first day of the week. Saturday and Sunday are weekend days. You can go to the park on those days. You can play with friends. The other five days are school days. You may have homework or chores to do on those days. Which day do you like best?

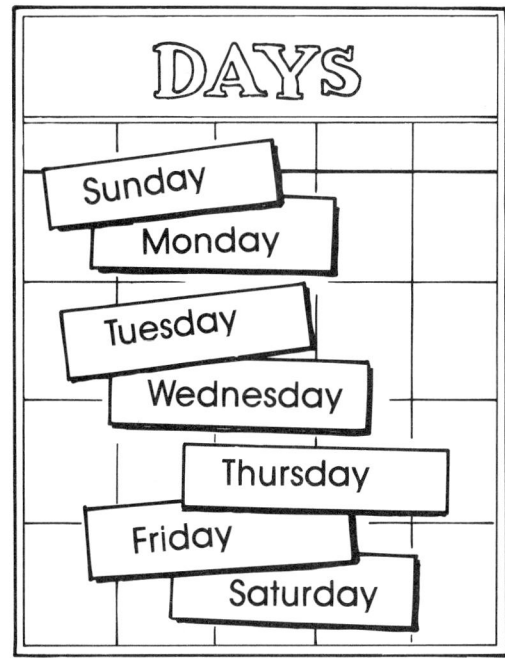

Circle the correct answer.

1. What day is a school day?

    A. Saturday

    B. Thursday

    C. Sunday

2. Which day is a weekend day?

    A. Monday

    B. Friday

    C. Saturday

3. Which day comes first?

    A. Sunday

    B. Tuesday

    C. Saturday

4. Which day do you like best? Write a sentence to tell why.

    _____
    _____
    _____
    _____

Name_____

Classifying

Read the story.

On the Go!

It is spring! It is time for the big picnic. But, how do all of the animals get there? Carla Caterpillar crawls. Bubba Butterfly flies. Freida Fish swims. Bertha Bee flies. Wanda Wolf walks. Fred Frog hops. Andrew Ant walks. Barsha Bunny hops. Willy Worm crawls. Sasi Sea Horse swims.

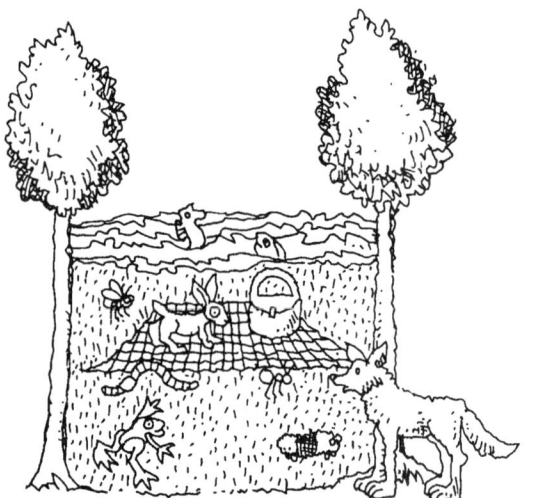

1. How does each animal get to the picnic? Cut out the pictures. Glue each animal in the correct place on the chart.

Walks	Crawls	Hops	Flies	Swims

   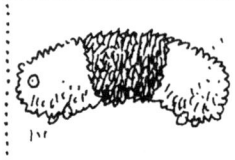 

 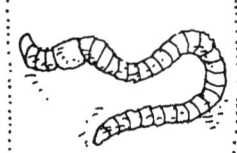   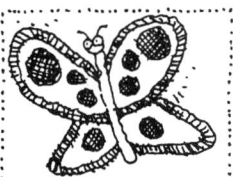

Name_____

Classifying

Read the story.

Taking Care of Fifi

Isabelle and Pete want to make money during the summer. They have looked for a long time to find jobs. Now, they have found a job they really like. Isabelle and Pete will take care of Fifi. Pete will take care of keeping Fifi clean and brushed. Isabelle will take care of feeding Fifi and giving her water.

1. What job do Isabelle and Pete have during the summer?

   _____

2. Help Isabelle and Pete get ready for their job. Cut out the pictures below. Glue the things Isabelle will need in her bone. Glue the things Pete will need in his bone.

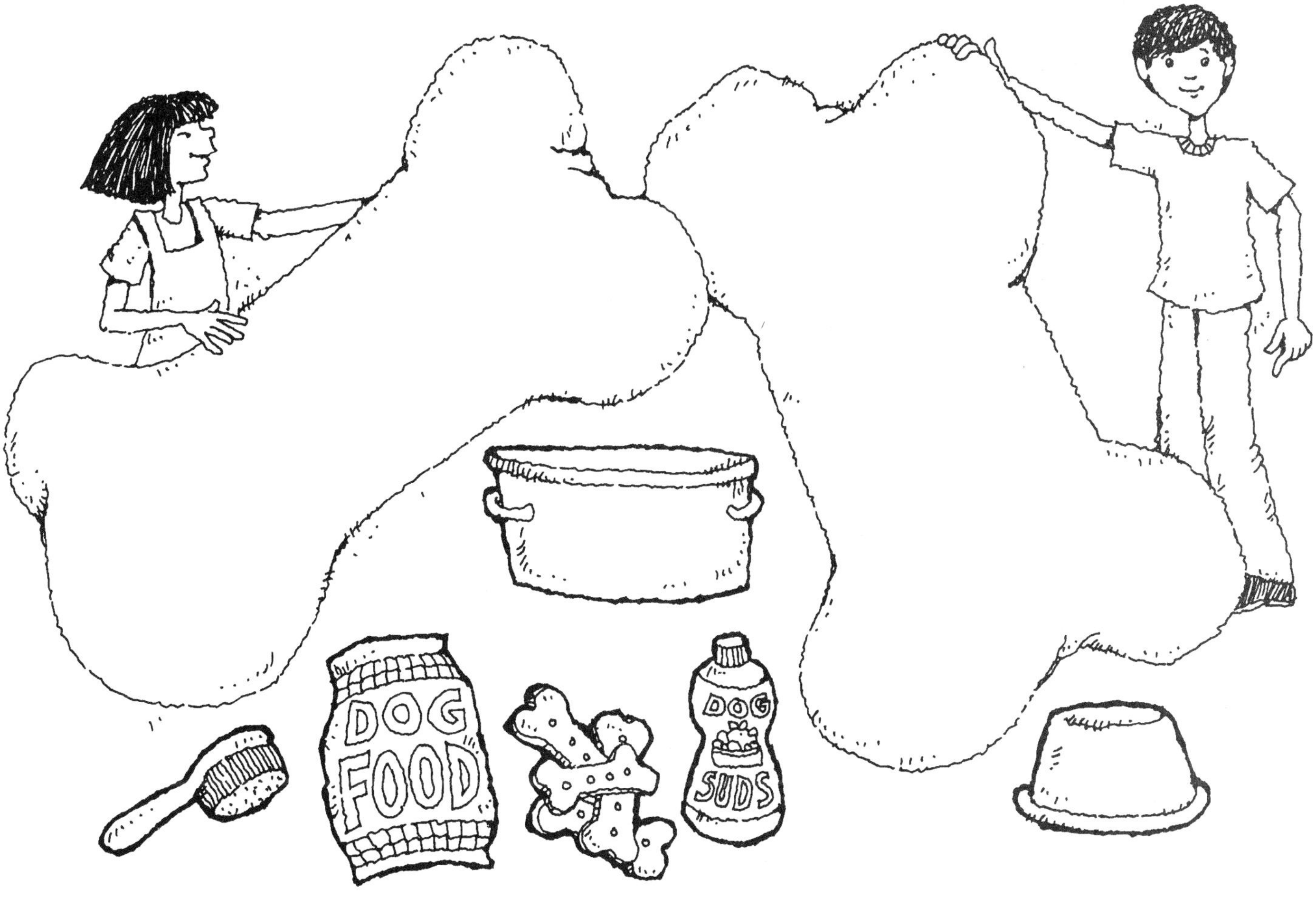

© Carson-Dellosa • CD-104839

Name_____

Classifying

Read the story.

My Feelings

Today, I had many feelings. I was happy when we had art class. I was sad when I heard a story about a hurt dog. When Ginny took my pen, I was angry. When my brother yelled "Boo!", I was surprised.

Draw a line to match each face to the correct feeling.

Write a word from the story to complete each sentence.

1.    A. sad

2.    B. happy

3.    C. angry

4.    D. surprised

5. When we had art class,

   I was _____.

6. When I heard the story,

   I was _____.

7. When Ginny took my pen,

   I was _____.

8. When my brother yelled,

   I was _____.

14 © Carson-Dellosa • CD-104839

Name_____

Classifying

Read the story.

Fruits and Vegetables

Dave's mother sells fruit. Dave loves to look at the red apples and the yellow bananas. He likes the peaches too. Dave's mother also sells vegetables. She sells carrots, corn, and potatoes. After school, Dave helps his mother at her store. He puts the fruits and vegetables into bags.

Look at each picture. Write **F** if it is a fruit. Write **V** if it is a vegetable.

1. _____

2. _____

3. _____

4. _____

5. _____

6. Circle the picture of something that Dave's mother sells.

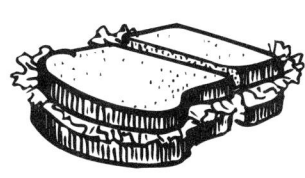 

Name_____

Classifying

Read the story.

Baby Animals

Baby animals sometimes have special names. A baby cat is called a **kitten**. A baby horse is called a **foal**. A baby cow is a **calf**. A baby dog is a **puppy**. How many baby animal names do you know?

Draw a line to match each animal to the correct name.

1.    A. calf

2.    B. puppy

3.    C. kitten

4.    D. foal

5. What is the main idea of this story?

_____

_____

Name_____

Classifying

Read about the stores on Main Street.

Shopping

Read each shopping list. Where should each person shop? Write the store number.

1. John needs eggs, milk, and bread.

   Where should John shop?

   Store Number _____

2. Sara needs dog food and a bird cage.

   Where should Sara shop?

   Store Number _____

3. José needs gum drops, candy bars, and jelly beans.

   Where should José shop?

   Store Number _____

4. Chang needs two pieces of pizza.

   Where should Chang shop?

   Store Number _____

5. Sally needs nails and a hammer.

   Where should Sally shop?

   Store Number _____

6. Ana feels sick.

   Where should Ana shop?

   Store Number _____

© Carson-Dellosa • CD-104839

Read the story.

Hats Off!

Kyle collects hats. He keeps his hats in boxes. Kyle's aunt came to visit. Kyle took his hats out of their boxes. He wanted to show them to his aunt. He sorted his hats. He lined them up.

Read about Kyle's hats.

Kyle has two big western hats.

Kyle has three baseball hats.

Kyle has one clown hat.

Kyle has two chef hats.

Finish drawing Kyle's hats.

Name_____

Classifying

1. Cut out the hats below. Glue each hat in the correct place on the chart.

Kyle's Hats

Number of Hats	Western	Baseball	Clown	Chef
4				
3				
2				
1				

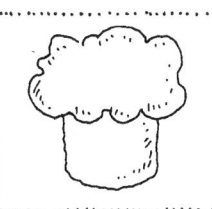
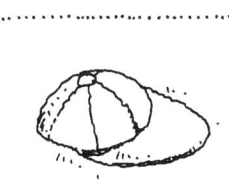
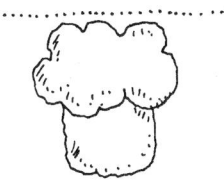
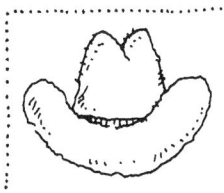

Name_____

Main Idea

Read the poem.

Kites

Kites can fly
On windy days,
Up in the sky,
In the sun's rays.
My kite can dance
Across the blue;
I feel so glad,
I could dance too!

Circle the correct answer.

1. What is the main idea of the poem?

   A. The sky is blue.

   B. I can run.

   C. Kites are fun.

2. Choose another title for this poem.

   A. The Sun's Rays

   B. Flying Kites

   C. Making Kites

3. What does "across the blue" mean?

   A. The kite is blue.

   B. The boy is sad.

   C. The sky is blue.

4. How does the author feel in this poem?

   A. sad

   B. glad

   C. mad

Name_____

Main Idea

Read the poem.

Letters

Letters, letters, all around!
They go from A to Z.
You use letters in your name
And for each word you see.
The letters of the alphabet
Are just like blocks for play.
You build your words
　with letters
And then read those words
　all day!

Read each sentence. Write **T** if it is true. Write **F** if it is false.

1. _____ The main idea of this poem is that letters make words.

2. _____ Another good title for this poem is "Talking All Day."

3. _____ Letters make names.

4. _____ Letters are like building blocks.

5. Write your first name.

　　_____

6. How many letters are in your first name?

　　_____

Name_____

Main Idea

Read the story.

Sun Bears

A sun bear is the smallest of all bears. It is black with an orange circle on its chest. The orange mark looks like a sun. That is how the sun bear got its name. Sun bears have long claws. These claws help them climb trees. Unlike most bears, sun bears live in trees. They build nests out of sticks. These small bears sleep all day and hunt at night.

Write a word to complete each sentence.

1. This story is about _____ bears.
2. The _____ mark on the bear looks like the sun.
3. Sun bears use their claws to help them climb _____.
4. Sun bears sleep all _____.
5. Sun bears build _____ out of sticks.
6. Sun bears hunt at _____.
7. What is the main idea of this story?

_____

_____

_____

Name_____

Main Idea

Read the story.

Pets

The students in Mrs. Beck's class talked about their pets.
Mona said, "My pet is Polly. She has green feathers. Her beak is sharp."
Luke said, "I keep my pet, Goldie, in a glass tank. She has a tail like a fan."
Javon said, "My pet, Slide, is long and thin. He slides along the ground."
Owen said, "My pet loves to wag his tail. His name is Sport."
Mrs. Beck said, "Everyone has a great pet!"

Write the name of each student next to the correct pet.

1.  This pet belongs to _____.

2.  This pet belongs to _____.

3. This pet belongs to _____.

4.  This pet belongs to _____.

5. Circle another title for this story.

   A. "Pet Care"

   B. "Great Pets"

   C. "Dogs Are Best"

   D. "I Love Birds"

Name_____

Main Idea

Read the story.

Teamwork

Animals can work in teams. Some small fish eat food from the teeth of big fish. Then, the big fish gets clean teeth!

Sometimes, animals help each other stay safe. One animal can do a good job of seeing. The other animal can do a good job of hearing. The animals stay close. One animal listens. The other animal watches.

Ants can get food from some small bugs. Then, the ants keep the small bugs safe from bigger bugs.

Animal teams can work well together.

Name_____

Main Idea

Complete each sentence with the correct answer.

1. This story is mostly about _____.

    bugs   ants   animal teams

2. Sometimes, small fish clean the teeth of _____.

    ants   big fish   bugs

3. Ants help keep small bugs safe from _____.

    bigger bugs   big fish   little fish

4. Animals can help each other stay _____.

    afraid   safe   bug

5. Draw your own animal team.

Name_____

Identifying Details

Read the story.

The New Puppy

Emma has a new puppy named Lucy at her house. Lucy is tan. Emma loves the puppy's soft fur and big black nose.

"Lucy is still a baby," Emma's mother says. "We need to feed her special food. She needs a warm bed too."

"I want to pet and play with her all of the time," says Emma.

"But, sometimes you have to leave Lucy alone," Emma's mother tells her. "She needs to rest and sleep. Soon, Lucy will want to play a lot of the time. But, not yet."

1. Use words from the story to complete the web.

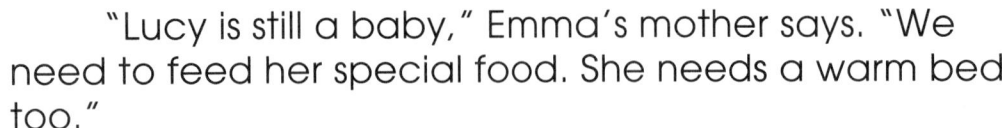

What Lucy Looks Like

_____

_____

_____

What Lucy Needs

_____

_____

_____

Name_____

Identifying Details

Read the letter.

A Letter to Julio

Dear Julio,

My dog's name is Nick. He is white with black spots. Nick likes to chase a ball. If I throw a ball, he can catch it in his mouth. When I go to school, Nick waits for me. When I come home, he is standing at the door. He jumps up and licks my face. Then, we go outside for a walk.

Your friend,
Fernando

Circle the correct answer.

1. Which dog is Nick?

   A.    C.

   B.

2. What detail helped you pick Nick?

   A. small with curly hair

   B. big with long brown hair

   C. white with black spots

3. What trick can Nick do?

   A. He jumps up and licks faces.

   B. He goes for a walk.

   C. He can catch a ball in his mouth.

4. What do Nick and Fernando do after school?

   A. They chase balls.

   B. They go for a walk.

   C. They wait for school to end.

Name_____

Identifying Details

Read the story.

Autumn

In autumn, the air gets cool. Students go back to school. Animals work hard to store food for the winter. Farmers store food too. They harvest their crops. People work in their yards and rake leaves. In many places, the leaves turn red, yellow, and orange. It is a pretty time of the year.

Use a word from the story to complete each sentence.

1. The air gets _____ in autumn.
2. Animals work to store _____ for the winter.
3. Farmers harvest their _____.
4. People work in their _____.
5. What is the main idea of this story?

_____

_____

_____

Name_____

Identifying Details

Read the story.

Ocean Food

People eat many things that come from the ocean. You have probably eaten several kinds of fish. Some people like shrimp. Others like clams and lobsters. People even eat plants from the ocean. Seaweed is one ocean plant some people like to eat. You may have eaten seaweed. One kind of seaweed is used to make ice cream!

Circle the correct answer.

1. What is this story mostly about?

   A. People eat some kinds of plants from the ocean.

   B. Some people like shrimp.

   C. People eat many things that come from the ocean.

2. Draw ocean animals and plants in the scene below.

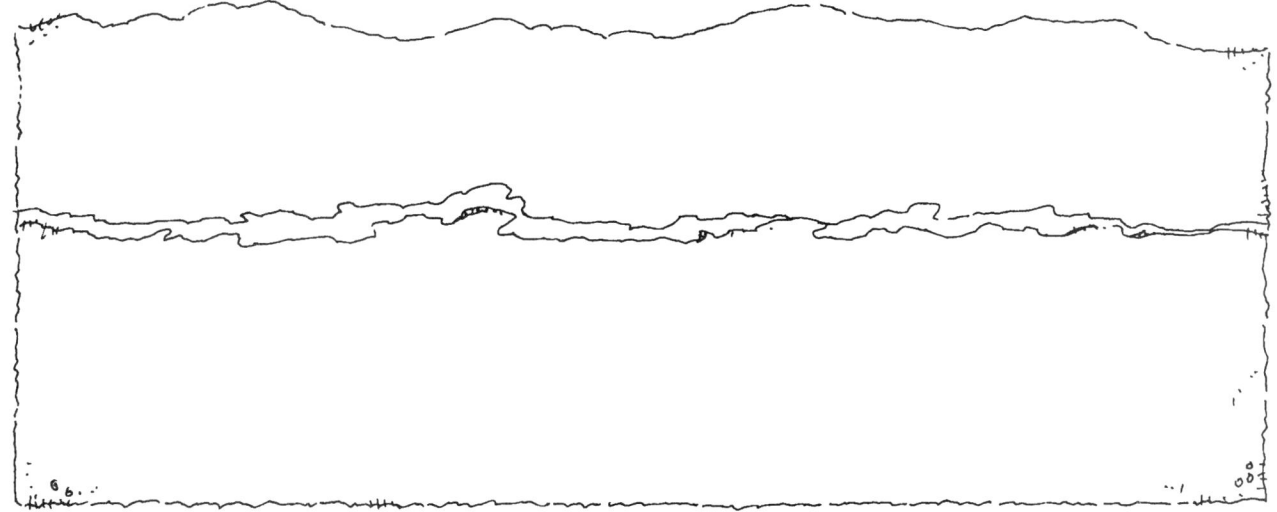

Read the story.

Picnic Poster

"I cannot believe the school picnic is next week," said Casey.

"Neither can I," said Tony. "That means summer is just around the corner. Do you want to make posters to tell everyone about the picnic?"

"Sure," said Casey. "What should the posters say?"

"They should let people know that the picnic will be on Sunday. That is May 25. And, it will be at Silas Park. Everyone should bring food. Be sure to sign your posters so that everyone will know that you made them."

1. Help Casey finish the poster for the picnic.

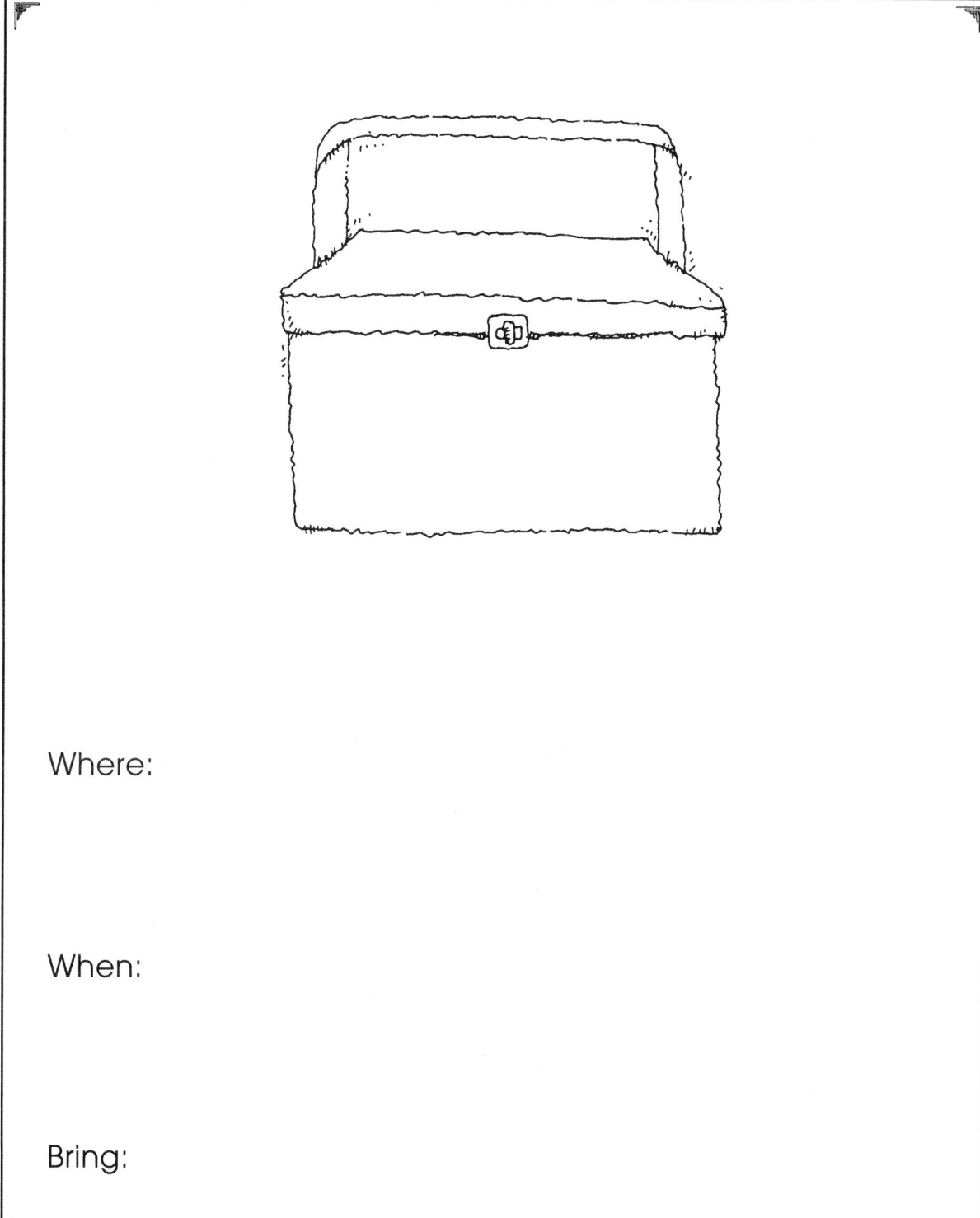

Where:

When:

Bring:

Name_____

Identifying Details

Read the story.

Party Mask

Ranita Raccoon wanted to go to a party. But, she needed a mask. So, she went to Brian Bear's Party Shop. "Why do you need a mask?" asked Brian Bear. "You already have one."

"Not really," Ranita answered. "All raccoons have a mask like mine. Will you help me find something different?"

"Sure," answered Brian. "Tell me about the mask you would like to wear."

"I would like a really big mask," said Ranita. "One with feathers. I would like it to be bright and shiny. And, I would like it to have a flag with two circles and two triangles."

"I can see you really know what you are looking for," said Brian. "Wait here. I will be back."

Identifying Details

1. Help Brian choose the mask for Ranita. Circle the correct mask.

2. Draw a mask you would like to wear to a party. Include details.

Name_____

Identifying Details

Read the story.

Time to Camp

Camping can be fun. But, it is important to prepare for a camping trip. You will need food and drinks. Bring marshmallows for a tasty treat. Be sure to take warm clothes for cool evenings. Your shoes should feel good on your feet. You will need a flashlight. Take a backpack that is not too heavy if you plan to hike. Do not forget your tent! Be sure it is set well into the ground. You do not want it to blow over in a strong wind!

Use a word from the story to complete each sentence.

1. Bring marshmallows for a _____ treat.
2. You will need a _____.
3. It is important to prepare for a _____ trip.
4. Your shoes should _____ good on your feet.
5. What is the main idea of this story?

_____

_____

Name_____

Identifying Details

6. Write a sentence that describes the main idea of the story on page 34 above the tent. Write three sentences that support the main idea on the tent.

Main Idea

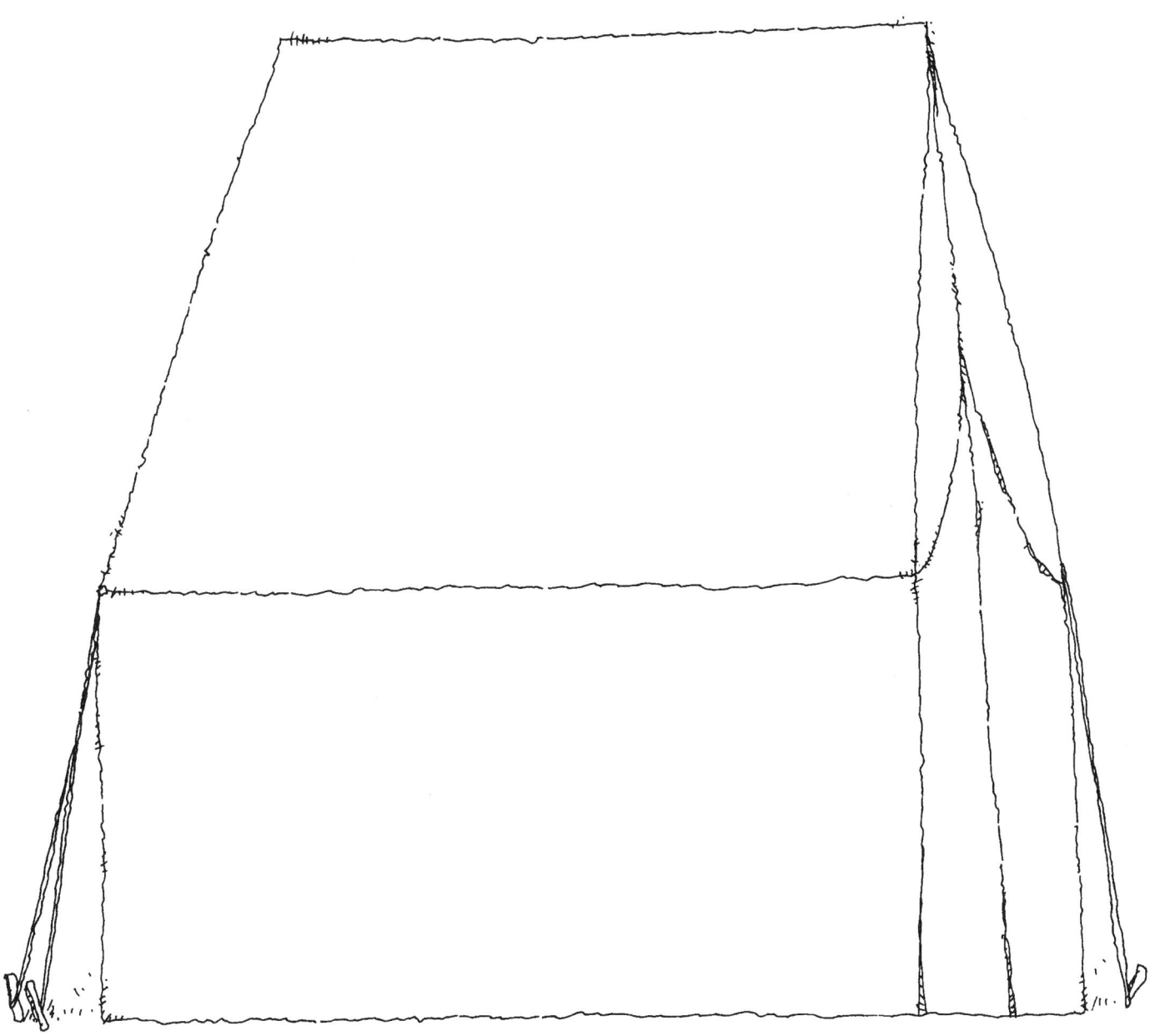

Read the story.

Whose Shoes?

"Happy birthday, Avery," shouted Carson. "You always have the best parties. What will we do next?"

"We can decorate our own shoes!" said Avery. He pulled five new pairs of tennis shoes from a bag.

Carson put rockets on her shoes. Avery put stripes on his. Lily drew circles all over her shoes. Mohammed glued shells on his. Reba glued stars on her shoes. Byron painted triangles on his. Avery and his friends put the shoes outside to dry.

Identifying Details

Name_____

Identifying Details

Draw a line to match each person to the correct pair of shoes.

1. Byron

2. Mohammed

3. Lily

4. Avery

5. Carson

6. Reba

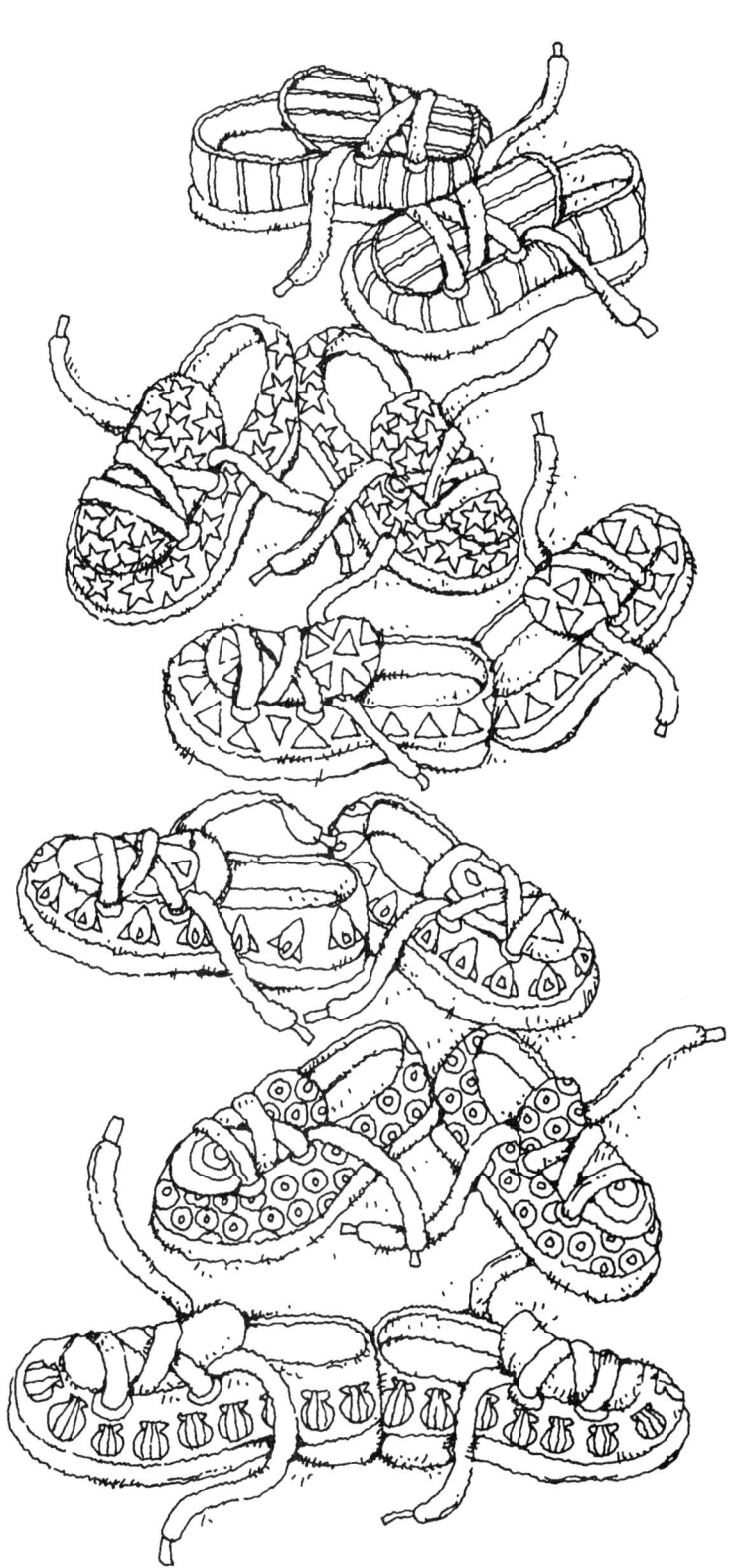

Name_____

Summarizing

Read the poem.

Points

Points on the needles,
Points on the nails,
Points on the starfish,
Points on the sails.

Points on the roofs,
Points on the bee,
Points on the playground,
Points for me!

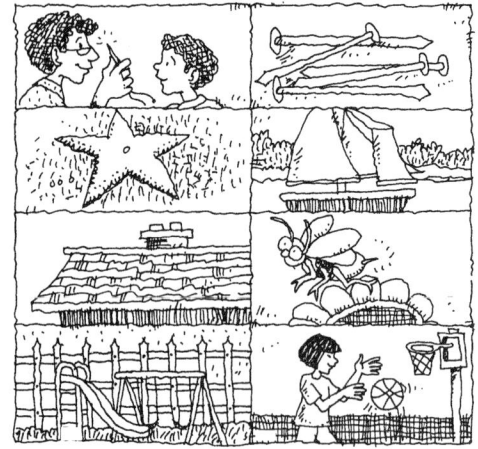

Answer the questions.

1. In your own words, tell what the poem is about.

   _____

   _____

2. How are the points in the last line of the poem different from the other points in the poem?

   _____

3. Which of the points in the poem is your favorite kind? Draw a picture to show your favorite.

Name_____   Summarizing

Read the story.

Clouds

Do you know where rain comes from? Rain comes from the clouds in the sky. Clouds are made of water. That water falls out of the clouds as rain. Sometimes, you can look at clouds and tell when it will rain. Clouds are white and puffy on sunny days. When it is going to rain, clouds turn gray.

Circle the correct answer.

1. Choose the sentence that tells about the whole story.

    A. Clouds are white and puffy on sunny days.

    B. Rain comes from clouds in the sky.

    C. Clouds can be gray or black.

2. Clouds are _____.

    A. always white and puffy

    B. gray on sunny days

    C. gray when it is going to rain

3. How can you tell if it is going to rain?

    A. by the water in the clouds

    B. by the sun

    C. by the color of the clouds

4. Circle the sentence that is true.

    A. Clouds are made of water.

    B. Rain comes from the air.

    C. Clouds are made of cotton.

Name_____

Summarizing

Read the story.

Seals

Seals swim in the ocean. They come to land to rest. Seals have shiny fur. They have big, dark eyes. Seals can see well under the water. Their favorite food is fish. Seals do not chew their food. They can eat a whole fish in one big gulp!

Answer the questions.

1. Describe what a seal looks like.

   _____

   _____

2. What is a seal's favorite food?

   _____

3. Where do seals go to rest?

   _____

4. Describe how a seal eats.

   _____

Name_____

Summarizing

Read the story.

The Earth

Earth is a planet. It revolves around the sun. This planet has everything we need to live. Earth has land and water. It gets light and heat from the sun. The heat keeps us warm. The light helps plants to grow. We breathe the air that surrounds Earth. We can grow food here. Earth is a good home.

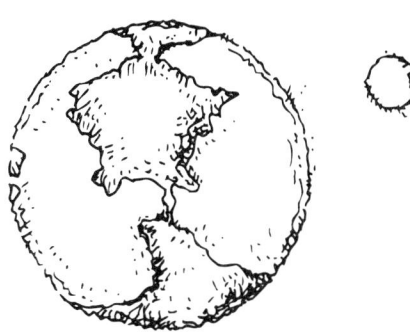

Circle the correct answer.

1. Earth is a _____.

    A. sun

    B. country

    C. planet

    D. land

2. This story tells us _____.

    A. why Earth is a good home for us

    B. how Earth revolves around the moon

    C. why Earth has air

    D. how Earth makes heat for itself

3. How does Earth get its light and heat?

    A. from the air

    B. from water

    C. from land

    D. from the sun

4. What are two important things Earth has that we need to live?

    A. air and water

    B. land and rocks

    C. light and heat

    D. toys and games

Name_____

Summarizing

Read the poem.

Go!

Wheelbarrow, wheelbarrow.
One wheel.
Go!

Scooter, scooter.
Two wheels.
Go!

Tricycle, tricycle.
Three wheels.
Go!

Skateboard, skateboard.
Four wheels.
Go!

Rocket ship, rocket ship.
No wheels.
Go!
ZOOM!

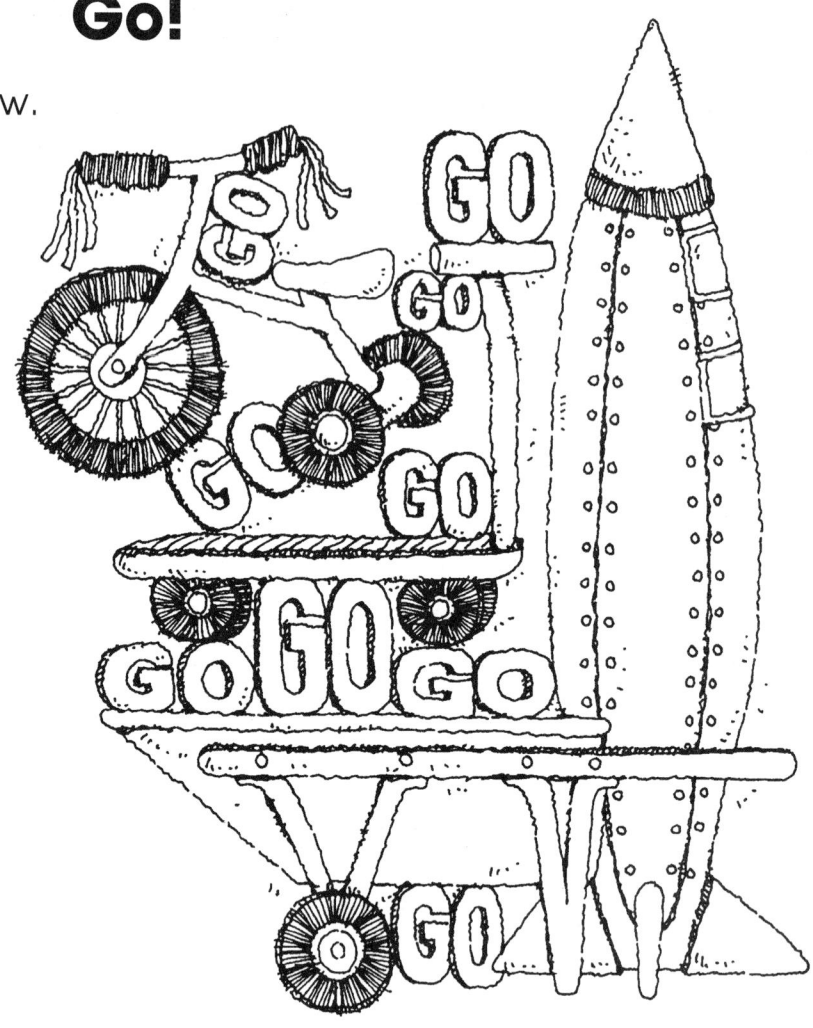

1. In your own words, tell what this poem is about.

   _____

   _____

   _____

   _____

2. Circle the word that shows how a rocket ship goes.

Read the story.

Winter Fun

Winter can be cold and snowy. People need to wear hats, coats, boots, and mittens to keep warm. In winter, it is fun to make snowmen. You need a carrot when you make your snowman. You also need coal. You can use a hat and a scarf to dress up your snowman.

Circle the correct answer. Use the picture to help you.

1. Why do people need to wear mittens in winter?

    A. to keep their heads warm

    B. to keep their hands warm

    C. to keep their toes warm

2. Why do you need a carrot to make a snowman?

    A. to make hands

    B. to make eyes

    C. to make a nose

3. Why do you need coal to make a snowman?

    A. to make a nose and buttons

    B. to make the eyes and buttons

    C. to make fingers and toes

4. Draw a hat on the snowman in the picture. Color the hat.

5. Have you ever made a snowman?

    Yes   No

Name_____

Context Clues

Read the story.

Bike Safety

No matter how old you are, there are rules to follow when you ride your bike. These rules keep bike riders safe. Riding a bike should be fun, but it is also important to know the rules.

Draw a line to match each safety rule to the correct picture.

1. Always ride in single file. A.

2. When you need to cross a street, walk your bike. B.

3. A bike with one seat should never have two riders. C.

4. Do what traffic lights and signs tell you to do. D.

44 © Carson-Dellosa • CD-104839

Name_____

Context Clues

Read the story.

All Kinds of Boats

There are many kinds of boats. A **rowboat** is a small boat that is moved with oars. **Oars** are long poles with wide, flat ends. A **tugboat** is a small, strong boat. It can push or pull boats that are much bigger. Another kind of boat is a **fireboat**. It puts out fires with water and hoses. A **sailboat** is moved by the wind. It has sails, which are made from strong cloth. The wind fills the sails and moves the boat through the water. A **houseboat** is a wide, flat boat with rooms where people can live.

Write the correct answer to each riddle.

1. I am moved by the wind. What am I?

   _____

2. I help put out fires. What am I?

   _____

3. I am moved with oars. What am I?

   _____

4. People can live in my rooms. What am I?

   _____

5. What kind of boat is this?

   _____

© Carson-Dellosa • CD-104839

Name_____

Context Clues

Read the story.

Parks

A park is a place for people to enjoy the outdoors. Most parks have lots of trees and flowers. People can sit on benches and enjoy the view. Children who come to the park can play on swings and slides. Sometimes people bring food to a park and eat at picnic tables. Parks are fun to visit.

Draw a line to match each word to the correct picture.

1. bench	A.

2. picnic table	B.

3. slide	C.

4. swing	D.

5. Why did the author write this story?

_____

_____

6. What is your favorite thing to do at a park?

_____

_____

Spider

1. Unscramble the words in the web.
   Write them on the lines.

   _____

   _____

   _____

   _____

   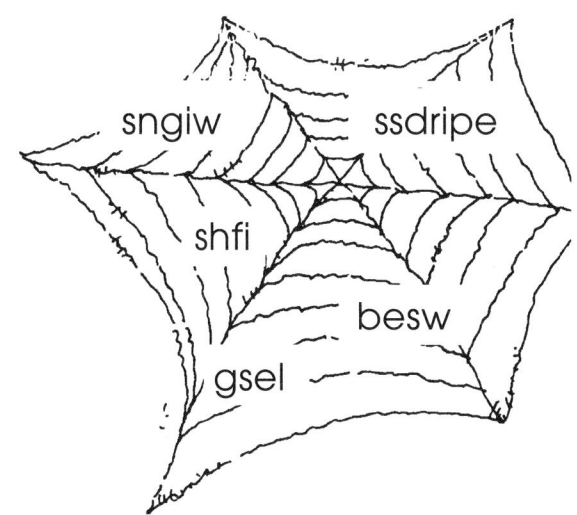

2. Use an unscrambled word to complete each sentence.

   Some people think _____ are insects. But, they are

   not. Insects have six legs. Spiders have eight _____.

   Spiders can catch insects that fly, but spiders cannot fly. They have

   no _____. Spiders spin their _____

   to catch food. Some spiders can go into the water. They catch little

   _____.

   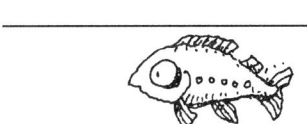

Name_____

Context Clues

Read the story.

What Makes You Special?

Each person is special. Each person does something well. Read about these special children. Jacob helps animals. Jayla does her best at sports. Denise recycles. Adam sings. Wyatt is an artist.

1. Draw a line to match each child's name to the correct picture.

Jacob

Jayla

Denise

Adam

Wyatt

2. Draw a picture and write a sentence to tell what makes you special.

_____

Name_____

Context Clues

Up, Up, and Away

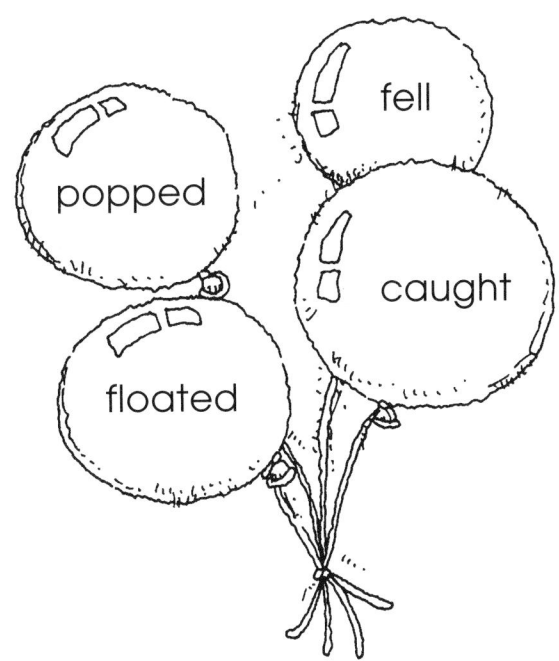

1. Use a word from the balloons to complete each sentence in the story.

Tracy and Sam went to the zoo. Whoops! Tracy let go of her balloon. Tracy's balloon _____ up into the sky. Sam shared his balloon with Tracy. Tracy said, "Thank you."

Sam dropped his ice cream cone. It _____ down to the ground. What a mess!

Tracy's grandpa held his balloon too close to the point on a fence. His balloon _____.

Sam's brother had a long string on his balloon. The string got _____ in a tree. Sam's brother could not get it loose. He had to get another balloon.

Name_____

Compare and Contrast

Read the story.

Flying the Friendly Skies

Airplanes have not always looked like they do today. The first planes had room for only one person, the pilot. Nothing covered the pilot's seat. Dirt blew into the pilot's face. There were no seat belts. Sometimes, pilots fell out of their planes! Airplanes have come a long way.

1. Write words in the chart to show how airplanes have changed.

First Planes	Planes Today

2. Draw a picture to show how you think planes will look in the future.

Name_____

Read the story.

Too Hot! Too Cold!

Sometimes, we feel too hot or too cold. When it is cold outside, we need to wear coats and boots to keep warm. When it is hot outside, we can go swimming or drink lemonade to cool off. There are many things we can do to feel better when we are too hot or too cold.

Circle the words **too hot** or **too cold** to finish each sentence.

1. I put on a  if I feel

   too hot.   too cold.

4. I put on my  when I feel

   too hot.   too cold.

2. I turn on a  if I feel

   too hot.   too cold.

5. I drink cold  when I feel

   too hot.   too cold.

3. I sit under a  when I feel

   too hot.   too cold.

6. I wear a  when I feel

   too hot.   too cold.

© Carson-Dellosa • CD-104839

Name_____

Compare and Contrast

Read the story.

Dinosaurs

Dinosaurs lived a long time ago. They all looked different. Some dinosaurs had horns and spikes. Some dinosaurs ate meat. Other dinosaurs ate plants. Most dinosaurs walked across the ground. A few dinosaurs could fly.

1. Write details from the story to complete the chart.

All Dinosaurs	
Dinosaurs Ate	**Dinosaurs Traveled By**

Name_____

Compare and Contrast

Read the story.

Wolves

Carmon tells her little sister, Ana, about wolves.

"Dog!" says Ana, pointing at the wolf picture.

"It is a wolf, not a dog," says Carmon. "But, dogs and wolves look alike. They are from the same animal family. A wolf can bark, just like a dog."

Ana points to the wolf's fur. "Soft," she says.

Carmon nods. "That is right. The wolf has soft, thick fur. It helps keep him warm. Wolves go hunting at night. Dogs are awake during the day. But, both wolves and dogs eat meat."

Read each sentence. Write **T** if it is true. Write **F** if it is false.

1. _____ Wolves and dogs can both bark.

2. _____ Dogs are awake during the day.

3. _____ Wolves go hunting during the day.

4. _____ Wolves eat meat, but dogs do not.

5. _____ Wolves and dogs are from the same animal family.

6. _____ Wolves and dogs do not look alike.

Name_____

Compare and Contrast

Read the story.

Trunks and Necks

Elephants and giraffes are alike because they are mammals. They are different because one has a long trunk and the other has a long neck. Elephants and giraffes both live in Africa. The elephant is gray, and the giraffe is tan and brown.

Both animals look for food when they are hungry. The elephant uses his long trunk to pick up grass, leaves, and other food and brings it to his mouth. The giraffe can eat leaves from tall trees because he has long legs and a long neck.

Name_____

Compare and Contrast

1. Use the words from the word bank to complete the Venn diagram.

lives in Africa	long legs	long trunk
a mammal	gray	tan and brown
long neck	picks up grass	looks for food

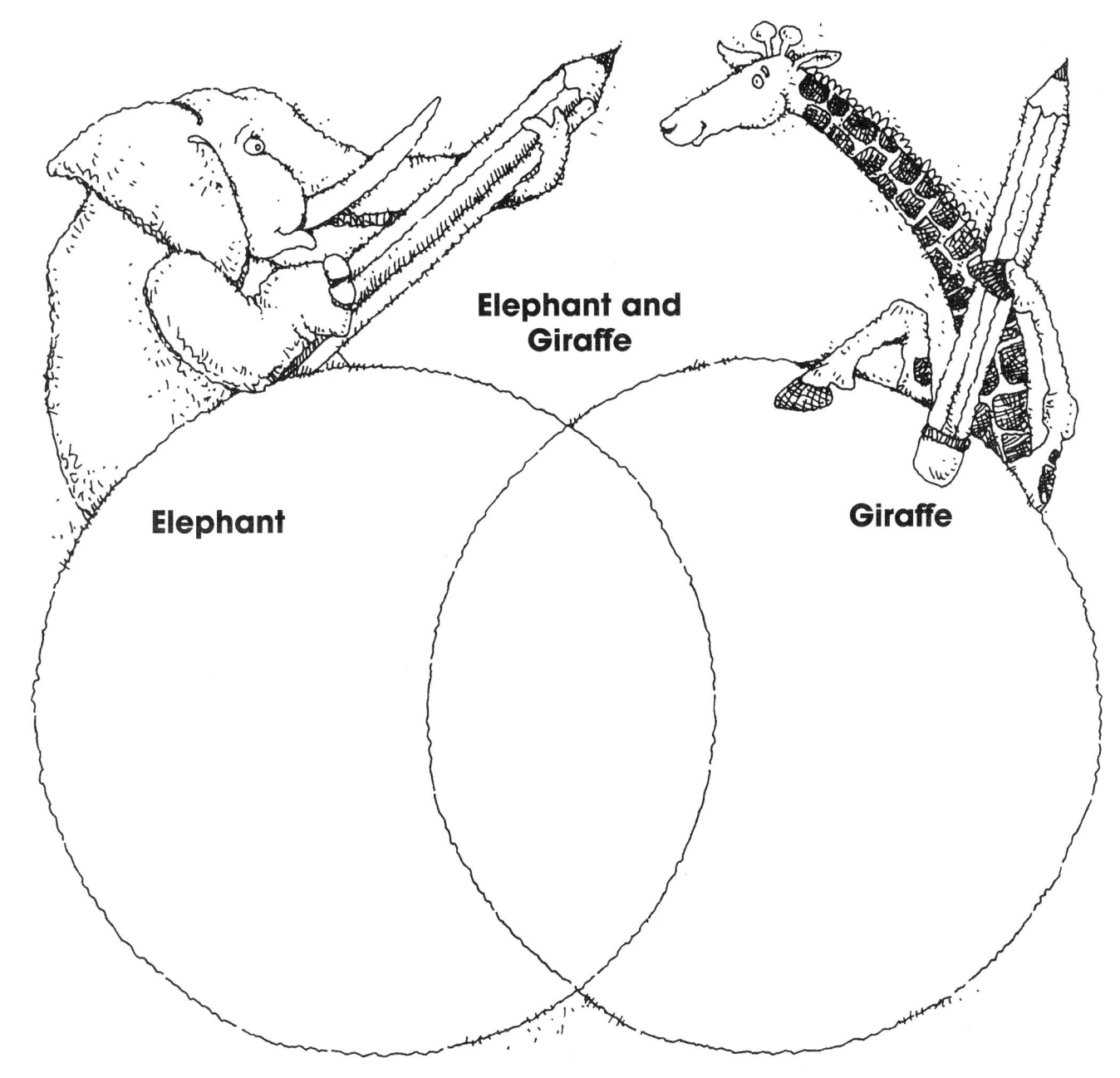

Read the story.

Ocean View

When you think of fish, do you think of fliers and rats? Flying fish and rat-tail fish both live in the ocean. Flying fish live near the top of the ocean. Rat-tail fish do not live near the top of the ocean. They live in deeper water.

Flying fish can swim. Rat-tail fish can swim too. Flying fish can jump a long way across the top of the water. Rat-tail fish cannot jump. Rat-tail fish have long tails. Flying fish do not have long tails. But, they have large fins like wings.

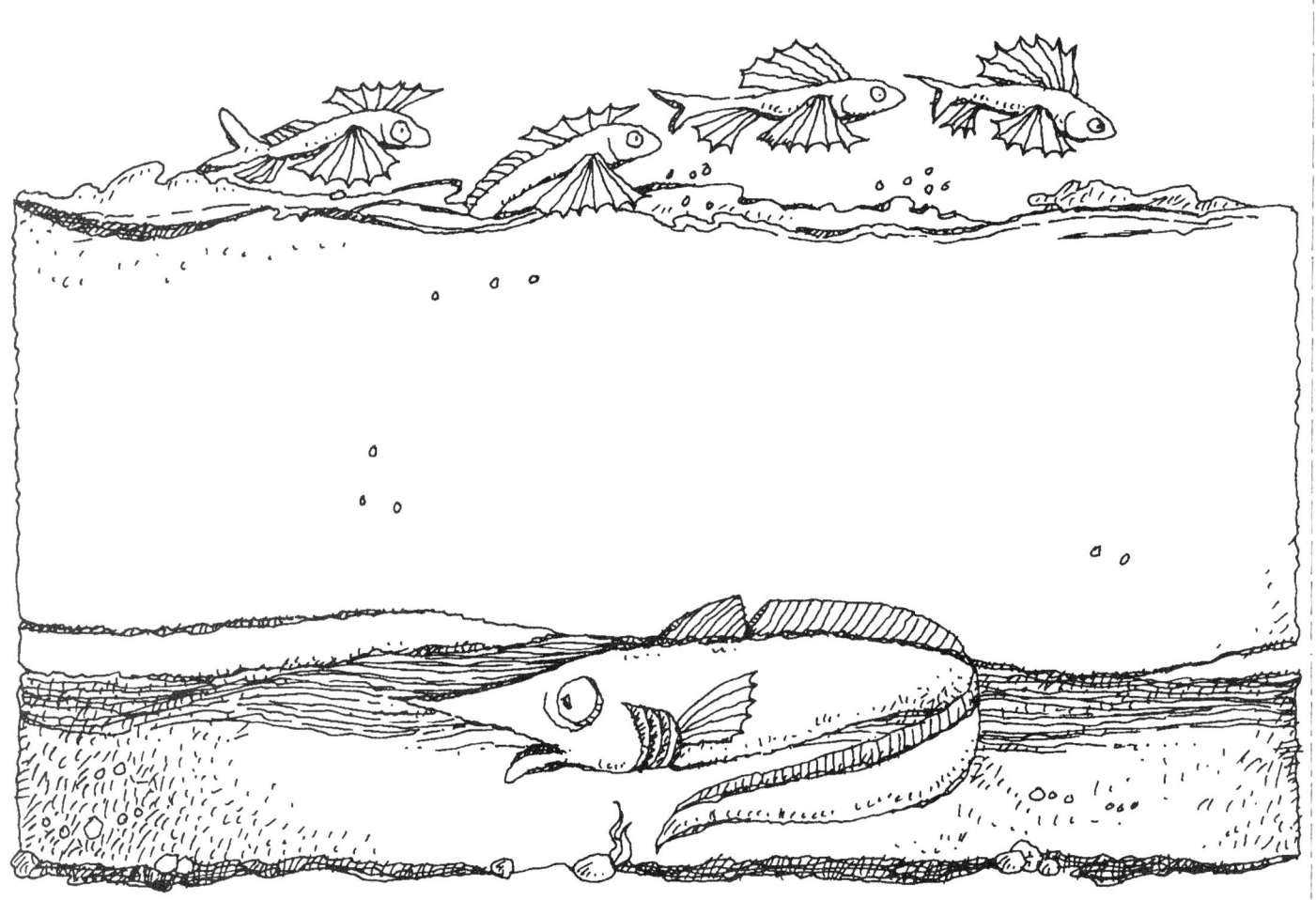

Compare and Contrast

1. Use words from the story to complete the Venn diagram.

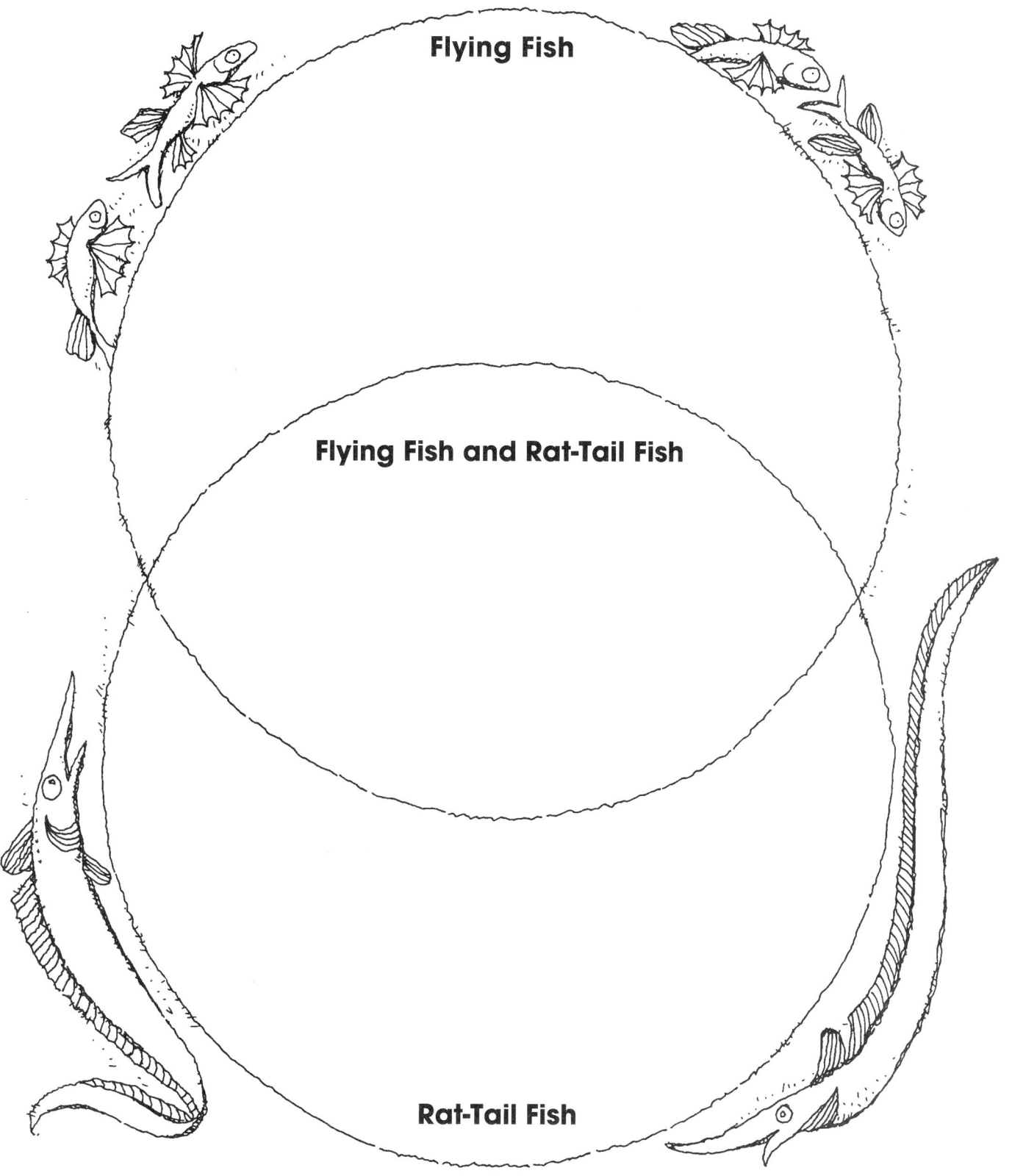

Name_____

Compare and Contrast

Read the story.

Where the Wild Things Live

What do the camel, the polar bear, the monkey, and the whale have in common? They are all mammals. But, each of these mammals lives in a different climate. The camel lives in places that are dry and hot. The polar bear lives in icy cold, snowy places. The monkey lives in jungles that are hot and wet. And, the whale lives in the ocean. Whales must live in water to stay alive.

1. How are the camel, whale, monkey, and polar bear alike?

    _____

2. How are the camel, whale, monkey, and polar bear different?

    _____

Name_____

Compare and Contrast

3. Draw a line to match each animal to the animal's climate.

camel   hot and wet

whale   hot and dry

polar bear   icy cold and snowy

monkey   ocean

4. Draw a picture to show each animal in the correct climate.

Camel	**Whale**
Polar Bear	**Monkey**

Name_____   Compare and Contrast

Read the story.

Zoo Riddles

Josh the zookeeper has to paint new signs for the zoo. Josh has decided to make his chore into a game. He has made up a riddle about each animal.

Read the riddle. Write the name of the animal on the line. Use the word bank to help you.

| giraffe | lion | seal | zebra |

1. I look like a horse, but I am black and white.

   If you tried to ride me, I would give you a fright!

   _____

2. I have a very loud roar and a mane.

   I am the king, I think that is plain.

   _____

3. I dive and swim, catch fish, and bark.

   My fur is shiny and very dark.

   _____

4. When I am hungry, I do not have to peck.

   I just reach to the trees with my long neck.

   _____

Name_____

Cause and Effect

Read the story.

The Sun

The sun is a big star. Earth is closer to the sun than to other stars. Because it is close, the sun gives us light. It keeps us warm. The light and warmth of the sun also help plants to grow.

It is nice to play outside on a sunny day. It is fun to fish and swim on a sunny day.

Write a word from the story to complete each sentence.

1. The _____ is a big star.

2. Because the sun is close, it _____ us light.

3. The light of the sun also keeps us _____.

4. What is the main idea of this story?

   _____

   _____

5. Draw a sun in the picture. Color it yellow.

Name_____

Cause and Effect

Read the story.

Traffic Signs

Traffic signs keep you safe. Some signs tell you to stop. Some signs tell you to go. When you do what the signs say, you stay safe. You help keep other people safe too.

Look at each sign. Write **Stop** or **Go** next to each picture.

1.  _____

2.  _____

3.  _____

4.  _____

5. What is the main idea of this story?

   _____

   _____

Name_____

Cause and Effect

Read the poem.

Wonderful Wheels

Did you ever think how it would feel
If nobody had invented the wheel?
No bikes, no wagons, no trucks or trains,
No cars to ride in ... not even planes!
Life would really be a bore
If wonderful wheels were no more.

1. Use words from the poem to complete the web.

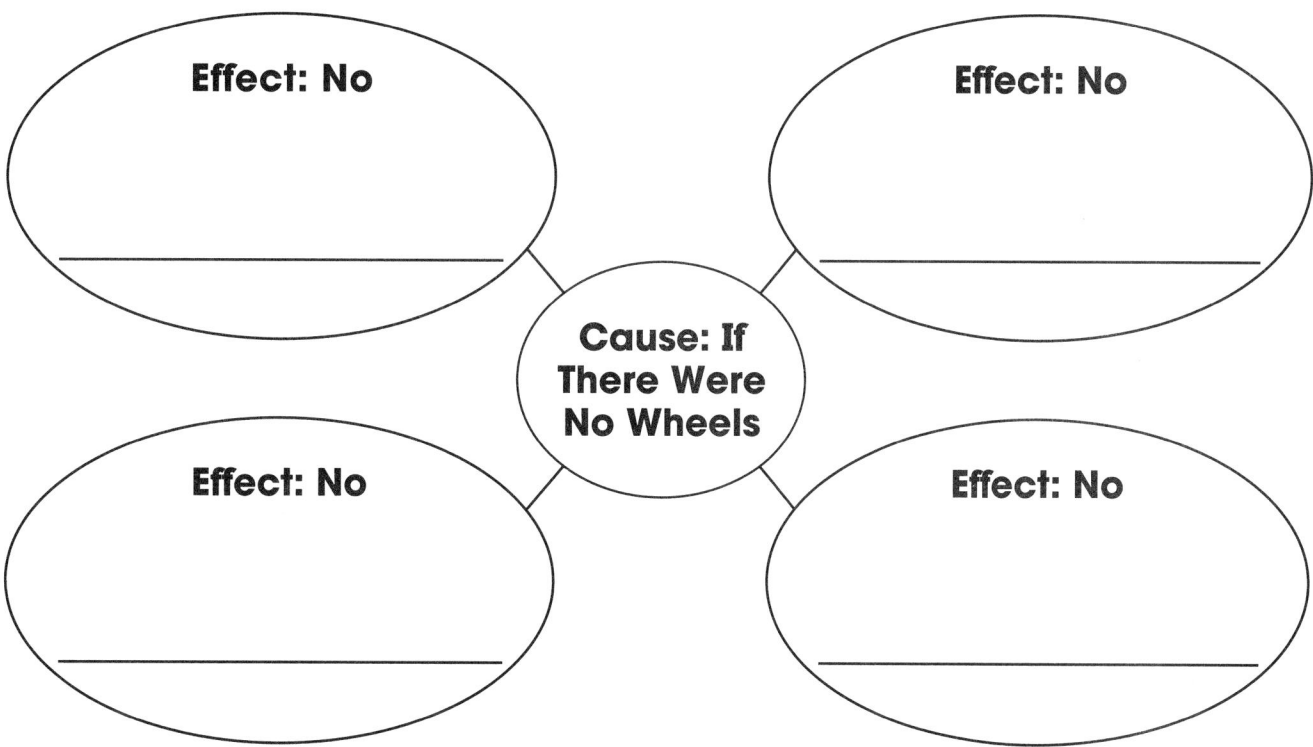

Read the poem.

Humpty Dumpty

Humpty Dumpty rode by a wall.
His horse tripped and made him fall.
On his way down, Humpty hit his
   head hard.
Could he be hurt? Friends ran
   to the yard.
But, Humpty was fine. "I am
   not hurt," he said.
"I wear a hard helmet on my
   egg head."

Draw a line to match each effect to the cause.

1. Friends ran to the yard   A. because his horse tripped.

2. Humpty was not hurt   B. because they wanted to see if Humpty was hurt.

3. Humpty fell   C. because his hard shell was like wearing a helmet.

4. What might have happened if Humpty did not have a hard shell?

_____

Name_____

Cause and Effect

Read the story.

Hummingbirds

Hummingbirds are the smallest birds in the world. They are also very fast. Hummingbirds flap their wings 50 times every second! The wings flap so fast that they make a humming sound. That is where the birds get their name. Hummingbirds must eat every 10 minutes. Hummingbirds' hearts beat very fast. They need a lot of energy from food just to keep their hearts beating to stay alive. Hummingbirds' beaks are long and pointed so that they can drink sugar from the centers of flowers.

Circle the correct answer.

1. Hummingbirds' wings make a humming sound because

   _____.

   A. their beaks are too long

   B. they flap their wings very fast

   C. they are in a hurry

2. Hummingbirds will eat every 10 minutes because they

   _____.

   A. need energy to stay alive

   B. are not hungry

   C. are so small

3. Hummingbirds can drink sugar from flowers because they

   _____.

   A. fly so fast

   B. have a fast heartbeat

   C. have a long, pointed beak

© Carson-Dellosa • CD-104839

Name_____

Cause and Effect

Read the story.

Pollution Solution

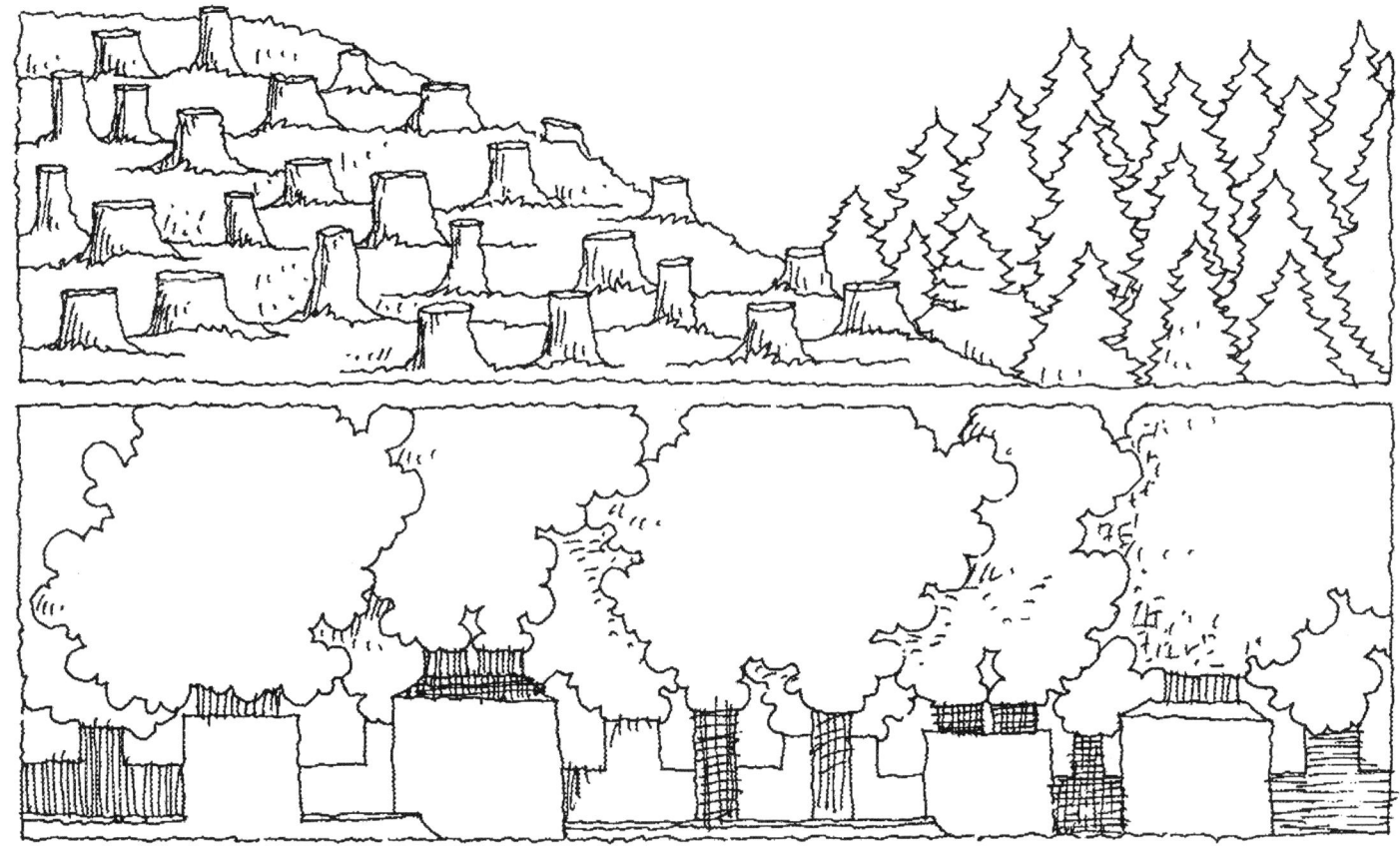

    Air pollution causes many problems. It makes air unsafe to breathe. Smoke causes air pollution. Smoke can put dangerous chemicals in the air. Cars cause air pollution. Cutting down too many trees is also bad for the air.

    What can people do to help stop air pollution and make the air safer? People can plant more trees. Trees can take away polluted air and help give fresh air. People can find a safer way to burn things. People can drive their cars less. People can make a difference.

Name _____

Cause and Effect

Answer the questions.

1. What does air pollution do to the air?
   _____
   _____

2. Name three things that can cause air pollution.
   _____
   _____
   _____

3. Name three ways people can help stop air pollution.
   _____
   _____
   _____

4. Draw a picture to show how you can help stop pollution.

Name_____

Cause and Effect

Read the story.

The Desert

A desert is a very dry land that gets little rain. The air is very hot in the daytime. At night, the desert becomes very cool. Some deserts are made of sand. The wind blows the sand into little hills called sand dunes. Only a few plants and animals can live in the desert.

Use a word from the word bank to answer each question.

| dry | hot | rain |

1. Only a few plants can live in the desert because there is not enough _____.

2. Some animals hide under rocks in the desert to stay cool because it is _____ in the daytime.

3. The desert is a very _____ land because it gets little rain.

4. What is the main idea of this story?

_____

_____

Name_____

Making Predictions

Read the story.

Trees

There are many kinds of trees. Some trees grow fruit. Other trees grow nuts. Some trees have flowers on them. All trees need sun and rain to grow.

Draw a line to match each sentence with the correct picture.

1. All trees need this to grow.   A.

2. Some trees grow fruit.   B.

3. Some trees have flowers.   C.

4. Some trees grow nuts.   D.

5. What is the main idea of this story?

_____

_____

Name_____

Making Predictions

Read the story.

Special Clothes

Many people wear special clothes, called uniforms, for their jobs. Uniforms help other people to know a person's job right away. Doctors, nurses, firefighters, and other helpers wear uniforms.

Draw a line to match each sentence to the correct person.

1. This person will help you if you smell smoke in your house.

   A.

2. This person will help you when you are sick.

   B.

3. This person will help you if your pet is sick.

   C.

4. This person can help you find a missing bike.

   D.

5. This person will help you mail a letter.

   E.

Name_____

Making Predictions

Read the story.

Going to the Doctor

Jason woke up one morning, and his head hurt. His mother said, "You feel hot. You better stay home from school."

Jason rested all day. He still did not feel good. His mother said, "You need to see the doctor."

The doctor took Jason's temperature. He looked in Jason's throat and his ears. Then, he said, "Jason, you need to do two things to get well."

1. Circle two things that Jason's doctor probably told him to do.

Name_____

Making Predictions

Read the story.

What is the Weather?

Every day, Mr. Benson's class reads a weather report from their pen pals on the Internet. This is today's report.

Circle the correct answer.

1. Who has sunny weather today?

   A. Sally and Matt

   B. Carla and Rosa

   C. Sally and Rosa

   D. André and Mike

2. Who has snow today?

   A. Mike

   B. Matt

   C. Rosa

   D. Carla

3. Who has rain today?

   A. Sally and Carla

   B. Mike and Carla

   C. Matt and Carla

   D. André and Carla

4. Who could fly a kite today?

   A. André

   B. Matt

   C. Mike

   D. Carla

Name_____

Making Predictions

What Happens Next?

One morning, Chris could not find his homework. He looked in his room. He looked in the kitchen. Then, he looked at his dog, Ruff. Ruff liked to hide things in his dog bed.

1. Where did Chris find his homework?

    A. in his room

    B. in Ruff's bed

    C. in the kitchen

2. What do you think Chris will do with his homework next time?

    A. put it next to Ruff's bed

    B. put it where Ruff cannot reach it

    C. give it to Ruff

Lee picks strawberries. He washes them well. He puts them in a bowl. He gets a spoon out of a drawer.

3. What will Lee do next?

    A. wash the strawberries

    B. go outside

    C. eat the strawberries

4. What did Lee do first?

    A. got a spoon out of the drawer

    B. washed the strawberries

    C. picked the strawberries

Name_____

Making Predictions

Read each rhyme.

Time to Rhyme

1. Circle the picture that shows what happens next.
2. Underline the words that show feelings.

Rover runs up.

Rover runs down.

Rover loves to run all around town.

Kim likes to fly

high in the sky.

It is vacation time!

I read every chance I get.

I love to grab a book.

It is one place where I love to go

To look and look and look.

Rain has fallen

all week long.

Must we stay inside?

Maybe we could go outside

and take a little ride.

Name_____

Making Predictions

Read the story.

Way to Grow!

Sean plants a vegetable garden. He plants his vegetables where they will get sunshine. He waters his vegetables. He feeds them plant food.

Robert plants a vegetable garden too. He plants his vegetables in a place with very little sunshine. He does not water his vegetables. He does not feed them plant food.

1. Draw what the vegetable gardens will look like this summer. Write the boys' names above their gardens.

2. What would you like to plant in a garden?

_____

_____

3. Draw a picture of your garden.

Name_____

Reality or Fantasy

Read the story.

Tigers

Tigers live in jungles. They are big animals with black stripes. Tigers are strong animals too. They have sharp claws and sharp teeth. Tigers are part of the cat family. They can climb trees. They can run very fast. They hunt for their food at night.

Circle the correct answer.

1. Which of these is not a real tiger?

   A.

   B.

   C.

2. Which of these do real tigers do?

   A. drive cars

   B. climb trees

   C. cut down trees

3. Which of these sentences is true?

   A. Tigers like to visit their cat cousins.

   B. Tigers shop for their food at stores.

   C. Tigers are part of the cat family.

4. Which of these sentences is not true?

   A. Tigers make good pets.

   B. Tigers are big animals.

   C. Tigers have black stripes.

   D. Tigers have sharp teeth.

Name _____

Reality or Fantasy

Read the story.

Chick and Duck

Chick thought that Duck was mad at him. Duck was sitting all by himself. Chick asked Duck what was wrong. He gave Duck treats and toys. At last, Duck said, "I am not mad. I just want to be alone for a while. We are still best friends."

Circle the correct answer.

1. Why did Chick think that Duck was mad?

   A. because Duck said he was mad

   B. because Duck was sitting by himself

   C. because Duck did not want the treats or toys

2. Why was Duck sitting alone?

   A. because he was mad

   B. because he did not like Chick

   C. because he wanted to be alone for a while

3. Which picture shows a real bird?

   A.

   B.

   C.

4. Where is one place you have seen a real bird?

   _____
   _____
   _____
   _____

Name_____

Reality or Fantasy

Read the poem.

If I Had Wings

If I had wings,
I would fly very high.
I would see everything
If I could fly!
I would fly to school,
And eat clouds for ice cream,
But I only fly
At night, in my dreams.

Answer the questions.

1. Can the person in the poem really fly?   Yes   No

   How do you know?

   _____

   _____

2. If the person in the poem could fly, what would she do?

   A. fly in the day

   B. fly to school

   C. fly to the moon

   D. fly to a party

3. If you could fly, where would you go?

   _____

   _____

Name _____

Reality or Fantasy

Read each sentence. Could the action in each sentence really happen? Circle **Yes** or **No**. If the sentence is fantasy, rewrite it to make it real.

Could This Be Real?

1. Sasha rode his  high in the sky. Yes   No

   _____

2. Tracy went to the  for a checkup. Yes   No

   _____

3. Anna and Sam played 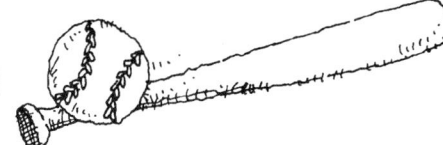 Yes   No

   _____

4. Riley rode all the way across the top of a  on her bicycle. Yes   No

   _____

Name_____

Reality or Fantasy

5. Draw two pictures. In one box, show something that could really happen. In the other box, show something that could not really happen.

Could Really Happen

Could Not Really Happen

Name_____

Reality or Fantasy

Read the poem.

Zuzu's Zoo

In a house whose color is blue,
Are lots of toy animals in Zuzu's zoo.
Some are small, like Ronnie Raccoon.
Others are big, like Betty Baboon.
Zuzu's bedroom is home to the zoo.
If you visit, she will show it to you.

Circle the correct answer.

1. Which animal might be in Zuzu's zoo?

    A.

    B.

    C.

3. Which sentence is true?

    A. Zuzu has a real zoo with real animals.

    B. Zuzu has a pretend zoo with toy animals.

    C. Zuzu has a real pet raccoon.

2. Which picture shows Ronnie?

    A.

    B.

    C.

4. What color is the toy animals' house?

    A. yellow

    B. blue

    C. red

Name_____

Fact or Opinion

Read the story.

Firefighters

A firefighter's job is to put out fires. This can be a dangerous job. Sometimes firefighters have to go into burning houses. Sometimes, they have to get people out safely. Whenever the bell rings, the firefighters rush to their truck. They wear special boots, hats, and coats to help keep them safe from the fire.

Read each sentence. Circle **F** if it is a fact. Circle **O** if it is an opinion.

1. F O   A firefighter's job is to put out fires.
2. F O   A firefighter's job is scary.
3. F O   Firefighters wear special clothes to help keep them safe.
4. F O   I would not want to be a firefighter.
5. F O   Firefighters rush to their truck when the bell rings.
6. F O   Firefighters drive a special truck.

7. What is the main idea of this story?

_____

_____

Name_____

Fact or Opinion

Read the story.

A Pet Story

Jenna has a dog. George has a cat. George thinks that cats are prettier than dogs. Jenna thinks that dogs are better pets than cats. One day, Jenna and George talked about the noises that their pets made. Cats meow. Dogs bark. They both agreed that dogs are louder than cats. George says that his cat is the best pet in the world. Jenna says that her dog is the best pet in the world. What do you think?

Circle the correct answer.

1. Which of these is a fact?

    A. Jenna has the best pet in the world.

    B. Cats are prettier than dogs.

    C. Dogs are better pets than cats.

    D. George has a cat.

2. Which of these is an opinion?

    A. Jenna has a dog.

    B. George's cat is the best pet in the world.

    C. Dogs bark.

    D. Cats meow.

3. Is a dog or a cat the best pet to have? Explain your opinion.

_____

_____

_____

_____

Name_____

Fact or Opinion

Read the story.

Sasha's Baby Brother

My new baby brother, Ty, is the loudest baby in the world. It seems like he never stops crying. He cries all day long. He cries just as I am falling asleep at night. Mom has to guess what Ty wants because he cannot tell us.

Sometimes, Ty stops crying. Then, he is the cutest baby in the world! He has black hair and dark brown eyes. He likes to wave his hands in the air. He has a great smile.

Read each sentence. Circle **F** if it is a fact. Circle **O** if it is an opinion.

1. F O Ty is the loudest baby in the world.

2. F O Ty is the cutest baby in the world.

3. F O Ty has black hair and dark brown eyes.

4. F O Ty likes to wave his hands in the air.

5. F O Ty cannot tell his family what he wants.

6. F O Ty should not cry so much.

7. Underline two words in the story that show feeling.

8. What is your opinion of babies? _____

_____

_____

Name_____

Fact or Opinion

Read the story.

It is a Fact! Or Is It?

Nelly Bly wanted to work for a newspaper in 1885. Many people thought women could not do this job. Nelly Bly asked a man for a newspaper job. The man thought women should not have jobs. But, Nelly Bly proved she could write. She got the job. She wrote many news stories.

1. Read each sentence. Write **F** in the newspaper if it is a fact. Write **O** if it is an opinion.

 Nelly Bly asked for a newspaper job.

 Women cannot do this job.

 Women should not have jobs.

 Nelly got the job.

2. Write one fact and one opinion about a family member.

Name_____

Making Inferences

Read the story.

The Post Office

The post office is the place that takes care of the mail. You can go there to mail your letters and packages. You pay to have your mail sent to other people. They pay to send mail to you. Some mail is sent far away. Mail is sent in many different ways. It can be sent on planes, trains, or trucks.

Circle the correct answer.

1. Which thing can you buy at the post office?

     A.

     B.

    C.

2. What is one way that mail is sent?

     A.

    B.

    C.

3. Which is something that you can mail?

     A.

    B.

    C.

4. What do you give the post office to send your mail?

     A.

    B.

    C.

Name_____

Making Inferences

Read the story.

New Gardens

Maggie and Zeb plant gardens. They buy seeds.

Here are Maggie's seeds.

Here are Zeb's seeds.

Circle the correct answer.

1. Aunt Susie wants to plant beans. Where will she plant them?

   A. in Maggie's garden

   B. in Zeb's garden

2. Where will Maggie put what she grows?

   A. in a tire

   B. in a vase

   C. in soup

3. What will Zeb be able to make from his garden?

   A. bread

   B. a book

   C. a salad

4. Circle the garden tools.

   A.

   B.

   C.

   D.

5. Would you rather plant a vegetable garden or a flower garden? Why?

   _____

   _____

Name________________________

Read the story.

Thank-You Letters

Michael had a birthday last week. He is writing letters to thank people for his gifts.

Read each one of Michael's letters. Then, circle the gift he got.

1. Dear Grandma,

   Thank you for your gift. Now, my hands will be nice and warm!

   Love, Michael

   A. 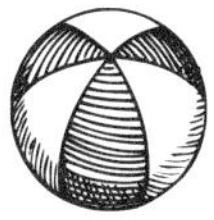

   B. 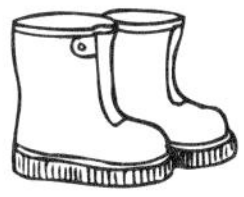

   C. 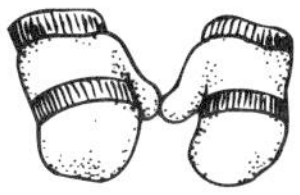

3. Dear Aunt Lee,

   Thanks for the birthday present. Now, I can pretend I am a cowboy!

   Love, Michael

   A. 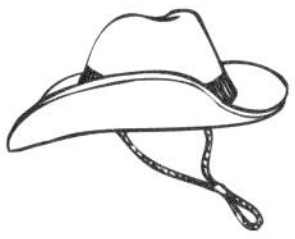

   B. 

   C. 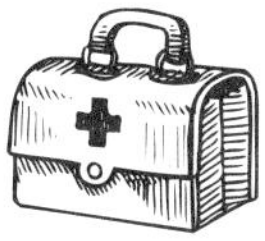

2. Dear Brad,

   We need to use your gift to play a game soon! Thank you.

   Your friend, Michael

   A. 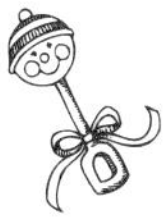

   B. 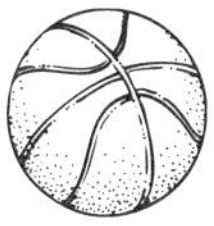

   C. 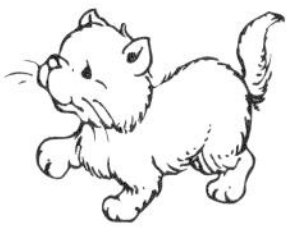

Name_____

Making Inferences

Read the story.

Riddle Time

When you read a riddle, you are playing a game to answer it. The riddle gives you clues. From the clues, you can guess what the riddle is about.

Draw a line to match each riddle to the correct picture.

1. I am orange and round. You can give me a grin.

    A.

2. I am sweet, but do not slip on my peel!

    B.

3. I am red and crunchy. Give me to your teacher.

    C.

4. Dig me up from the ground. You can make fries from me!

    D.

5. Write your own riddle.

_____
_____
_____
_____
_____

Name_____

Making Inferences

Read the story.

Rain, Rain, Go Away

Crash! Boom! It rained. Oliver painted a picture. He played with his yo-yo. He played a game with his grandpa.

Oliver waited for the rain to stop. He saw the sun. "Grandpa," he said. "Let's go outside. Let's go find it!" Oliver and his grandpa ran outside. They looked up at the sky. They looked and looked.

Answer the questions.

1. Why was Oliver playing inside?

   _____

2. What did Oliver and his grandpa want to find? Circle **Yes** or **No** for each sentence.

They were looking for snails.	Yes	No
They were looking for worms.	Yes	No
They were looking for a rainbow.	Yes	No
They were looking for cats and dogs.	Yes	No

Name_____

Story Elements: Character

Read the story.

Dolly

Dolly the Dolphin has a job. She works at Ocean Land. People come to Ocean Land to see fish and other sea animals. Dolly knows how to do tricks. She swims very fast. Dolly works with a trainer to learn new things. She knows how to ask for treats. Dolly lives in the water, but she is not a fish. She is a mammal. Dolly needs air to live. She comes to the top of the water to get air.

Draw a line to complete each sentence.

1. Dolly is a   A. works with a trainer.

2. Dolly knows how to   B. very fast.

3. To learn new things, Dolly   C. dolphin.

4. Dolly is not   D. do tricks.

5. Dolly can swim   E. a fish.

6. Where does Dolly work? _____

Name_____

Story Elements: Character

Read the story.

The Basketball Player

Anna held her breath as the ball sailed up to the hoop. It went in! Anna had helped win the game! The tall, thin girl cheered with her team. Her black hair fell in her eyes as she jumped up and down. Anna saw her mom and dad in the crowd. They waved and smiled. She felt happy and proud.

1. Use words from the story to complete the web.

Anna's Height
_____

Anna's Hair Color
_____

All about Anna

Anna's Sport
_____

How Anna Feels
_____
_____

Read the story.

Too Big

Barker wished she was the biggest dog on the block. Every time Barker saw Bruiser, she hung her head. I will never be that big, she thought. What good is a little dog? A big dog can carry newspapers. She can chase away pesky cats. She can do it all. And, I cannot do anything.

One day, Barker padded along the sidewalk. "Help," someone cried. Barker ran to check out the problem. Bruiser stood nearby.

"A boy is caught in the bushes on the other side of the wall," Bruiser said. "There is a small hole, but I cannot get through."

Barker trotted through the hole. She tugged on the branches wrapped around the child's ankle. She got the boy free. "Thank you," cried the boy. The boy hugged Barker and patted her head.

Barker licked the boy's face. Barker saw Bruiser looking through the hole. Bruiser said, "Good job, Barker." Barker wagged her tail.

Name_____

Story Elements: Character

Think about how Barker changes in this story.

1. Circle the paw that shows how Barker feels at the beginning of the story.

2. Write a word that tells how Barker feels at the beginning of the story.

3. Circle the paw that shows how Barker feels at the end of the story.

4. Write a word that tells how Barker feels at the end of the story.

5. Why do Barker's feelings change at the end of the story?

_____
_____
_____
_____

Name_____

Story Elements: Character

Read the story.

The Farmer

Mason is a farmer. He has an important job. He grows food that we eat. Mason grows wheat and oats. He also takes care of the animals on his farm. Mason works hard. He gets up early every day. He works until it is dark. He loves helping the young plants grow. He smiles as he works. In the fall, he harvests his crops. The wheat is made into bread. The oats are made into cereal.

Circle the correct answer.

1. How do you know that Mason works hard?

    A. He grows wheat and oats.

    B. He gets up early and works late.

    C. He has an important job.

2. How do you know that Mason likes being a farmer?

    A. He smiles as he works.

    B. He harvests his crops.

    C. He grows oats for cereal.

3. What happens to the wheat that Mason grows?

    A. It is made into cereal.

    B. It is made into dinners.

    C. It is made into bread.

4. Why is Mason's job important?

    A. Farmers smile as they work.

    B. Farmers grow the food we eat.

    C. Farmers work hard.

Name_____

Story Elements: Setting

Read the poem.

Up and Away

I fasten my belt and close my eyes.
The next time I look, we are up in the skies!
Mom reads her book, but I look outside.
I feel like a bird on this airplane ride.
Blue sky above and white clouds below.
I look out the window and watch the show!

Circle the correct answer.

1. How is this child traveling?

   A.

   B.

   C.

3. What does the child see below?

   A.

   B.

   C.

2. What does the child do first?

   A.

   B.

   C.

4. Where must the child be sitting?

   A.

   B.

   C.

Name_____

Story Elements: Setting

Read the story.

At the Airport

An airport is a busy place. It is where planes take off and land on runways. People line up to buy tickets for the planes. Their bags are driven to the planes in open trucks. The airport has places where you can eat and buy gifts. You can buy a book to read on your flight. There are also places with big windows where you can watch the planes land.

Draw a line to match each sentence to the correct picture.

1. A plane takes off on the runway.

    A.

2. People buy tickets for the planes.

    B.

3. People can eat at the airport.

    C.

4. Bags are taken to the planes in open trucks.

    D.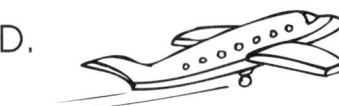

5. What is the main idea of this story?

   _____
   _____
   _____

Story Elements: Setting

Read the poem.

My Favorite Place

My favorite place is a wonderful store.
If you would like, I'll tell you more.
There are cases of dolls,
Tiny beds, little chairs.
There are shelves full of animals—
Stuffed mice and stuffed bears!

Read each sentence. Write **T** if it is true. Write **F** if it is false.

1. _____ This poem is about a clothing store.

2. _____ The bears are on shelves.

3. _____ The tiny beds and little chairs are for dolls.

4. _____ Stuffed animals are sold in this store.

5. _____ The poem says that the store sells toy trains.

6. _____ The mice in the poem are real.

7. _____ The poem says there are only a few dolls.

8. Circle the word that describes the store.

Name_____

Story Elements: Setting

Read each story. Draw a line to match each story to the picture that shows the correct time and place.

So Many Places

1. "Good morning, Mom," said Jimmy as he raced down the stairs. "What time do we leave for vacation? I can hardly wait!"

2. "The lake is the best!" said Ashton. She leaned against a tree. "I really like it when the sun starts to go down. I am ready to tell scary stories."

3. The submarine moved deep in the ocean. Ross saw fish and an octopus outside the window. He looked at his watch. "It is so dark down here, it does not seem like four o'clock," he thought.

4. "Brrrr! It is so cold here on top of the mountain in the middle of the night." Shelby pulled her hat down over her ears. Soon, it would be time to go back down the mountain.

Name _____

Story Elements: Setting

5. Choose one of the settings from page 100. Write your own story in that setting. Draw a scene from your story below.

_____

_____

_____

_____

_____

_____

Name_____

Story Elements: Plot

Read the story.

A Trip to the Farm

I am so excited! Today, I get to visit Aunt Jenna.

Aunt Jenna has a farm. When I visit her, I get to pet all of the animals. Aunt Jenna lets me bake cookies. We pick vegetables from her garden. We plant flowers.

I am packing my suitcase. It will be a great trip!

Draw a line to match the words to the correct picture.

1. pet the animals   A.

2. bake cookies   B.

3. pick vegetables   C.

4. plant flowers   D.

Name_____

Story Elements: Plot

Read the story.

Sharing

Wendy was Taylor's baby sister. Wendy wanted to do everything that Taylor did. Taylor was going to eat the last piece of cake. But, there was a problem. Wendy wanted to eat a piece too. Taylor had an idea. She cut the piece of cake in half. The two sisters ate their snack together.

Circle the correct answer.

1. Which one is Taylor?

    A.

    B.

    C.

2. What did Wendy want to eat?

    A.

    B.

    C.

3. Who is Wendy?

    A. She is Taylor's cousin.

    B. She is Taylor's cat.

    C. She is Taylor's sister.

4. How did Taylor fix her problem?

    A. She shared the cake.

    B. She put Wendy to bed.

    C. She threw away the cake.

Name_____

Story Elements: Plot

Read the story.

A Strange Meeting

Terry was sitting by the river. He felt a bump on the back of his shell. An owl had landed on him!

"Excuse me," said Terry. "Would you please move?"

"Oh!" said Olive Owl. "I am so sorry. I thought you were a rock."

Olive flew to a tree. Terry pulled his head inside his shell and went to sleep.

Answer the questions.

1. What kind of animal is Terry? _____

2. What animal landed on Terry's shell? _____

3. Was Olive Owl polite or rude? _____

4. Why do you think Olive thought Terry's shell was a rock? _____
_____
_____

5. What did Terry do at the end of the story? _____
_____

Name_____

Story Elements: Mixed

Read the story.

Riding Bikes

Cari and Raul wanted to ride bikes together. They were going to ride to the playground. But, when Cari went to get her bike, she had a problem. Her bike had a flat tire.

"Do not worry," said Raul. "Walk your bike to my house. My mom can fix the tire for you."

Circle the correct answer.

1. Which picture shows what was wrong with Cari's bike?

    A.

    B.

    C.

2. Find the picture that shows where Cari and Raul wanted to go.

    A.

    B.

    C.

3. How was Cari's problem solved?

    A. Raul's mom would fix the tire.

    B. Raul fixed the tire.

    C. Cari's mom fixed the tire.

4. What probably happens after the bike is fixed?

    A. Cari and Raul eat a snack.

    B. Cari and Raul go to the playground.

    C. Cari will go back to her house.

Name_____

Story Elements: Mixed

Read the poem.

Animal Friends

Big Bear, Little Bear, Silver, and Woof
All live with me under one roof.
They are my friends. They sleep on my bed.
They never need walking or need to be fed.
I tell them my secrets, and they never speak.
They do not make a sound, not even a squeak.

Circle the correct answer.

1. What is this poem about?

    A. animals who live in the woods

    B. toy animals on a girl's bed

    C. pets who live in a kennel

2. What kind of animal do you think Woof is?

    A. a real dog

    B. a toy dog

    C. a toy horse

3. What is the setting for the poem?

    A. in a kitchen

    B. in a garage

    C. in a bedroom

4. How are these animals different from real pets?

    A. They are friends.

    B. They sleep on a bed.

    C. They never need to be fed.

Name_____

Story Elements: Mixed

Read the story.

A News Story

Today, a young girl told the police that her sheep were lost. She did not know where to find them. The police officer told the girl to leave the sheep alone. He was sure that the sheep would come home by themselves.

Circle the correct answer.

1. Who is the young girl in the story?

    A. Little Miss Muffet

    B. Goldilocks

    C. Little Bo-Peep

2. What is the girl's problem?

    A. She cannot find her house.

    B. She cannot find her sheep.

    C. She cannot find her dog.

3. What did the police officer tell the girl?

    A. to go looking for the sheep

    B. to ask people if they had seen the sheep

    C. to leave the sheep alone

4. How do you think this story will end?

    A. The sheep will come home.

    B. The sheep will stay lost.

    C. She will find the sheep herself.

Name_____

Story Elements: Mixed

Read the poem.

Trisha's Pet

Cat
Shy, green-eyed
Purring, yawning, sleeping
Tiger

Circle the correct answer.

1. Who is Tiger?

    A. a jungle animal

    B. Trisha's cat

    C. a pet dog

2. What kind of cat is Tiger?

    A. shy and friendly

    B. mean and hissing

    C. brave and noisy

3. Which of these probably tells what Tiger looks like?

    A. a black cat with yellow eyes

    B. a white cat with blue eyes

    C. a striped cat with green eyes

4. What else can you tell about Tiger from the poem?

    A. He likes to take naps.

    B. He likes to hunt outside.

    C. He likes to eat fish.

Name_____

Following Directions

Read the director's stage directions.

Under the Sea

"Take your places, glub, glub," says Dolphin Director. "Starfish, put on a purple scarf and swim over to the table. Crab, you will be the queen. Put on a gold crown and crawl to the center of the stage. Sea Horse, tie a red bow around your tail. Float over to the mirror. Eel, wrap yourself around the pole to give us light." Dolphin Director takes his place beside the curtain.

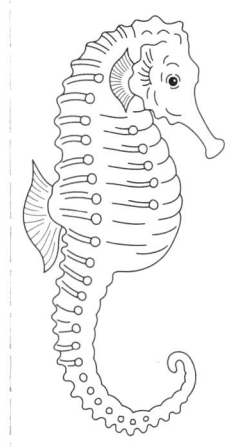

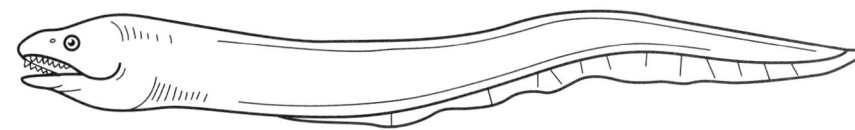

Draw and color each animal in the correct place.

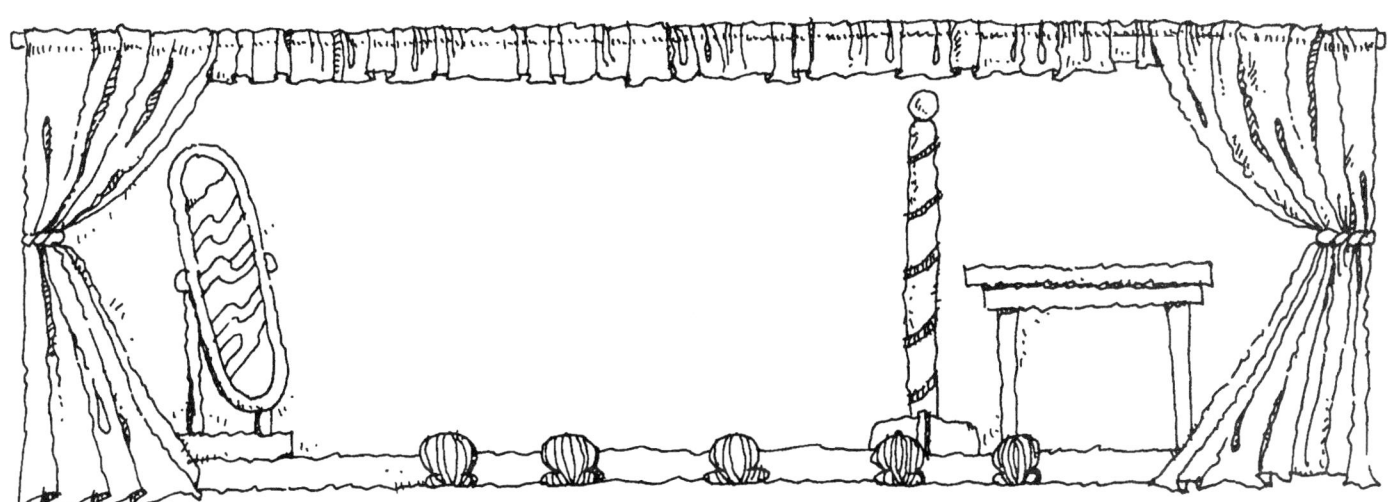

© Carson-Dellosa • CD-104839

Name_____

Following Directions

Read the story.

Riddle Around

    I am round. I have a net under me. I have a board behind me. Players jump near me. Players throw something orange and round through me. What am I?

1. Circle the word that answers the riddle.

   fishing pole   basketball   hoop   lake

2. Draw a basketball over the basketball hoop.

   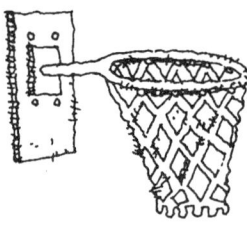

3. Draw a net under the basketball hoop.

   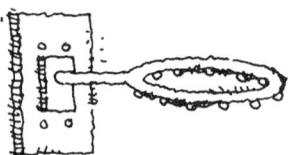

4. Draw a backboard behind the basketball hoop.

   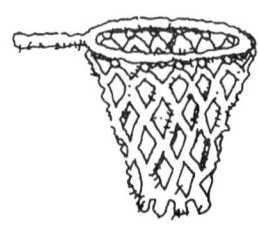

Name_____

Following Directions

Read the story.

Elephant Gardens

Eli Elephant has two gardens. He has a flower garden and a vegetable garden. Eli waters his gardens with his trunk.

Follow the directions to give Eli's gardens more color.

1. Color the pond blue.
2. Color Eli gray.
3. Use a pencil to draw water coming from Eli's trunk to water the gardens.
4. Color the short flowers purple.
5. Color the tall flowers orange.
6. Draw a green circle around the vegetable garden.

Use the words from the word bank to complete the song.

The Wheels on the Bus

down   people   round   town   wheels

The _____ on the bus go round and round,

round and round,

round and round.

The wheels on the bus go round and _____ all through the town.

The _____ on the bus go up and down,

up and down,

up and down.

The people on the bus go up and _____

All through the _____.

Name_____

Cloze

Use the words from the word bank to complete the song.

Twinkle, Twinkle

| are | sky | star | up | wonder |

Twinkle, twinkle little star,

How I wonder what you _____!

_____ above the world so high,

Like a diamond in the _____.

Twinkle, twinkle little _____,

How I _____ what you are!

Name_____

Cloze

Use words from the word bank to complete each rhyme.

Rhyme Time

crown　　　down　　　fiddle　　　moon　　　spoon

Jack and Jill

Jack and Jill went up the hill
To fetch a pail of water.

Jack fell _____ and broke his _____,
And Jill came tumbling after.

Hey Diddle, Diddle

Hey diddle, diddle,

The cat and the _____,

The cow jumped over the _____.

The little dog laughed
To see such a sport,

And the dish ran away with the _____!

Choose one of the rhymes and draw a picture of it.

What Do They Grow?

Write the correct word on each line.

Who grows grapes?

Grace _____ grapes.

Who grows green beans?

Greg _____ green beans.

Who grows grain?

Grey grows _____ .

Who eats Grace's _____

and Greg's _____ _____

and Grey's _____ ?

A greedy green grasshopper eats them all!

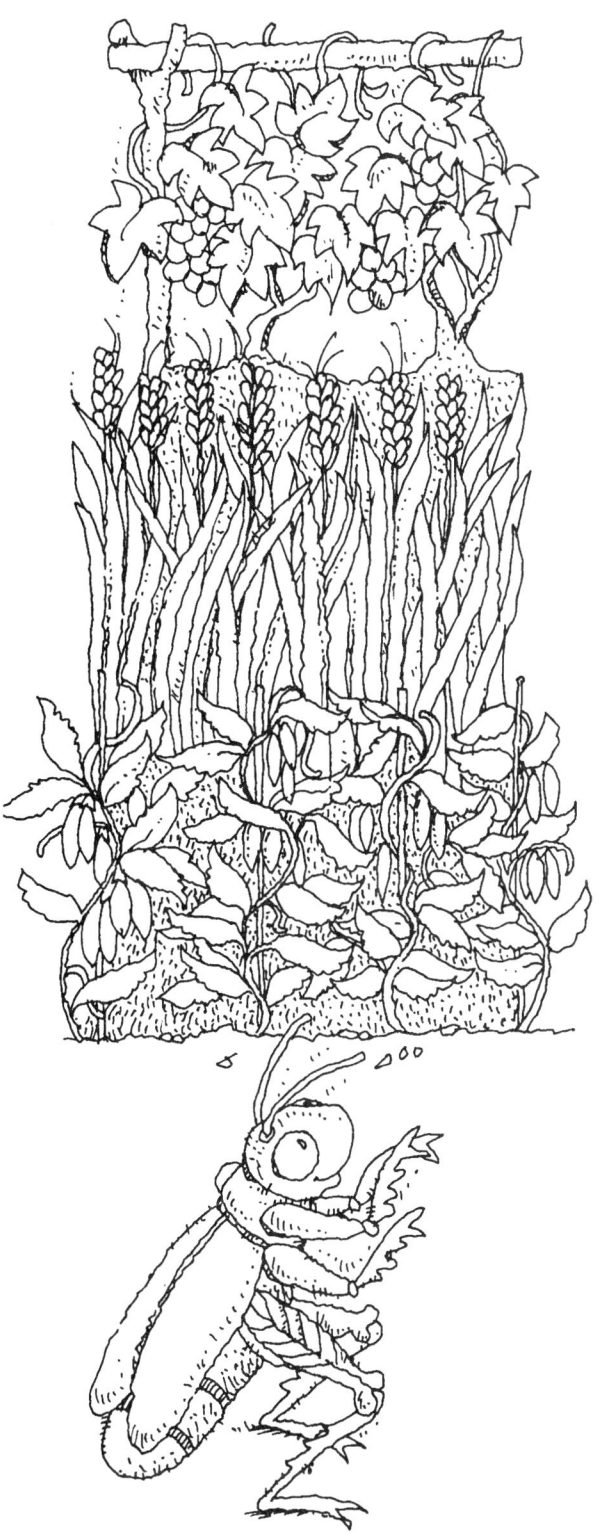

Name_____

Generalizing

Read the story.

Long Ago

Dinosaurs lived long ago. All dinosaurs are extinct today. Not all dinosaurs were large. Some were as small as chickens. Some dinosaurs ate other animals. Many dinosaurs ate only plants. No people lived when dinosaurs were alive.

Use a word from the word bank to complete each sentence.

All	Many	No	Some

1. _____ dinosaurs were as small as chickens.

2. _____ dinosaurs are extinct today.

3. _____ people lived when dinosaurs were alive.

4. _____ dinosaurs ate only plants.

5. Draw a dinosaur picture.

Name_____

Generalizing

Read the story.

Feathered Friends

How are all birds alike? They all have feathers. They all lay eggs. All birds are reptiles. How are some birds different? Some birds live in caves. They can fly in the dark. And, they still know where they are going. Most birds live outside caves. They like to soar in the sky.

Use a word from the word bank to complete each sentence.

All	Most	No	Some

1. _____ birds can fly in the dark.
2. _____ birds have feathers.
3. _____ birds are mammals.
4. _____ birds live outside caves.

5. What is the main idea of this story?

_____

_____

_____

Read the story.

In the Rain Forest

What do ants, parrots, monkeys, tree frogs, and snakes have in common? You can find them all in the rain forest. Some of these animals, like monkeys, are mammals. Others, like parrots, are birds. A tree frog is an amphibian you can find in the rain forest. Reptiles, such as snakes, can be found there too. Ants are insects that crawl in the rain forest. These animals come in many colors. They live by eating many different things.

Use words from the story to complete the chart

Animals	Kind of Animal
parrot	_____
_____	insect
jaguar	mammal
_____	reptile
_____	amphibian
monkey	_____

Name_____

Charts and Graphs

Use the picture to help you answer each question.

1. Which two animals are mammals?
   _____

2. Which animal is a reptile?
   _____

3. Which animal is an insect?
   _____

4. What is another insect you might find in the rain forest?
   _____

Read the story.

Candy

Candy is a favorite sweet-tasting food. The main ingredient of most candy is sugar.

There are four main types of candies. They are made differently and contain different things. The best-selling candy is chocolate. The most popular chocolate candies are solid chocolate and chocolate-covered candy bars.

Hard candy is also popular. This candy starts out as a liquid that is boiled. Flavoring and color are added. Then, as it cools, it is shaped. A favorite hard candy is the candy cane. These used to be mostly made with peppermint, but now fruit and chocolate flavorings are also used.

Chewy candies are candies such as caramels. These are cooked, cooled, and then cut into pieces or poured into molds and allowed to set.

Whipped candies are nougats and marshmallows. These are syrups that are mixed with air. Marshmallow bunnies and chickens are examples of these.

Take a survey. Ask your friends about their favorite kinds of candy. Gather your information using the four main types of candies in the story. Use what you learn to fill in the bar graph on page 121.

Name_____

Charts and Graphs

1. Make a bar graph to show the results of the survey you took.

Favorite Types of Candy

	1	2	3	4	5	6	7	8	9	10	11	12	13
Chocolate Candies													
Hard Candies													
Chewy Candies													
Whipped Candies													

2. What kind of candy did the most amount of people like?

   _____

3. What kind of candy did the least amount of people like?

   _____

4. Were there any types of candy that tied or were close?

   _____

Just for fun, try asking the same number of just girls, just boys, or just adults, and see if the results are the same.

Name_____

Charts and Graphs

Read the story.

State Birds

Every state has a state bird, flower, and tree. Here are some examples. The seagull is the state bird for Utah. Seagulls eat crickets that kill the crops grown there. The state tree for Vermont is the sugar maple. Vermont makes maple syrup from these trees. The state flower in Virginia is the flowering dogwood. These flowers bloom on the dogwood tree every spring. You can find each state's tree, flower, and bird by using books in your library.

This chart lists five state birds and their states. Use the chart to answer the questions.

1. What is Michigan's state bird?

   _____

2. What is Louisiana's state bird?

   _____

3. How many states have the cardinal as the state bird?

   _____

4. Which state has the purple finch as its state bird?

   _____

Answer Key

Page 5
1. B; 2. C; 3. A; 4. The bus helps people.

Page 6
1. A; 2. C; 3. B; 4. tracks

Page 7
1. 2, 3, 1; 2. hot day; 3. Answers will vary. 4. How to make an ice cream cone.

Page 8
1. C; 2. B; 3. C; 4. Answers will vary.

Page 9
1. A; 2. B; 3. A; 4. B

Page 10
1. C; 2. B; 3. C; 4. Answers will vary.

Page 11
1. B; 2. C; 3. A; 4. Answers will vary.

Page 12
1. Walks: wolf, ant; Crawls: caterpillar, worm; Hops: frog, bunny; Flies: butterfly, bee; Swims: fish, sea horse

Page 13
1. Isabelle and Pete take care of Fifi.
2. Isabelle's bone: dog food, dog biscuits, dog dish; Pete's bone: dog brush, dog shampoo, large tub

Page 14
1. B; 2. D; 3. A; 4. C; 5. happy; 6. sad; 7. angry; 8. surprised

Page 15
1. V; 2. V; 3. F; 4. V; 5. F; 6. Banana should be circled.

Page 16
1. B; 2. C; 3. D; 4. A; 5. Baby animals have special names.

Page 17
1. 3; 2. 5; 3. 4; 4. 2; 5. 1; 6. 6

Page 18
Check students' drawings.

Page 19
Chart will contain two western hats, three baseball hats, one clown hat, and two chef hats.

Page 20
1. C; 2. B; 3. C; 4. B

Page 21
1. T; 2. F; 3. T; 4. T; 5–6. Answers will vary.

Page 22
1. sun; 2. orange or circle; 3. trees; 4. day; 5. nests; 6. night; 7. give information about how sun bears look and live

Page 23
1. Javon; 2. Owen; 3. Mona; 4. Luke; 5. B

Page 25
1. animal teams; 2. big fish; 3. bigger bugs; 4. safe; 5. Drawings will vary.

Answer Key

Page 26
1. What Lucy Looks Like: tan, soft fur, big black nose; What Lucy Needs: special food, warm bed, rest/sleep

Page 27
1. B; 2. C; 3. C; 4. B

Page 28
1. cool; 2. food; 3. crops; 4. yards; 5. things people can do in the fall

Page 29
1. C; 2. Drawings will vary.

Page 31
1. Where: Silas Park, When: Sunday, May 25; Bring: food; Poster should include Casey's signature.

Page 33
1. Correct mask: big mask with feather, sequins, and flag with two circles and two triangles. 2. Drawings will vary.

Pages 34–35
1. tasty; 2. flashlight, backpack or tent; 3. camping; 4. feel; 5. It is important to prepare for a camping trip. 6. Answers will vary but may include Main Idea: It is important to prepare for a camping trip. Supporting Details: Bring marshmallows. Bring a flashlight. Wear shoes that feel good on your feet.

Page 37
1. shoes with triangles; 2. shoes with shells; 3. shoes with circles; 4. shoes with stripes; 5. shoes with rockets; 6. shoes with stars

Page 38
1. Answers will vary but should reflect understanding of difference in meaning of points at end of the poem. 2. The points for the author of the poem are not real objects. 3. Drawings will vary.

Page 39
1. B; 2. C; 3. C; 4. A

Page 40
1. Seals have shiny fur and big, dark eyes. 2. fish; 3. land; 4. Seals eat fish in one big gulp.

Page 41
1. C; 2. A; 3. D; 4. A

Page 42
1. Answers will vary. 2. ZOOM

Page 43
1. B; 2. C; 3. B; 4. Hat should be drawn and colored in the picture. 5. Answers will vary.

Page 44
1. B; 2. C; 3. D; 4. A

Page 45
1. sailboat; 2. fireboat; 3. rowboat; 4. houseboat; 5. tugboat

Page 46
1. D; 2. B; 3. A; 4. C; 5. to tell what people can do at parks; 6. Answers will vary.

Page 47
1. spiders, legs, wings, webs, fish; 2. spiders, legs, wings, webs, fish

Answer Key

Page 48
1. Jacob: boy feeding cat, Jayla: girl holding soccer ball, Denise: girl putting can into recycling bin, Adam: boy looking at sheet music, Wyatt: boy sitting next to sculpture handling clay; 2. Drawings and sentences will vary.

Page 49
1. floated, fell, popped, caught

Page 50
1. First Planes: room for only one person, no cover for pilot's seat, dirt blew into pilot's face, no seat belts, pilots sometimes fell out of planes; Planes Today: room for many people, plane seats have covers, pilots do not fall out, dirt does not blow into pilot's face, planes have seat belts. 2. Drawings will vary.

Page 51
1. too cold; 2. too hot; 3. too hot; 4. too cold; 5. too hot; 6. too cold

Page 52
All Dinosaurs: lived long ago, did not look the same; Dinosaurs Ate: meat, plants; Dinosaurs Traveled By: flying, walking

Page 53
1. T; 2. T; 3. F; 4. F; 5. T; 6. F

Page 55
1. Elephant: long trunk, gray, picks up grass; Both: mammal, looks for food; Giraffe: long neck, tan and brown, long legs

Page 57
1. Flying Fish: live near top of ocean, do not have long tails, can jump; Both: live in ocean, can swim; Rat-Tail Fish: live deep in the ocean, have long tails, cannot jump

Pages 58–59
1. All of these animals are mammals. 2. All of these animals live in different climates. 3. camel: hot and dry; whale: ocean; polar bear: icy cold and snowy; monkey: hot and wet; 4. Drawings will vary.

Page 60
1. zebra; 2. lion; 3. seal; 4. giraffe

Page 61
1. sun; 2. gives; 3. warm; 4. to tell how the sun helps people and plants; 5. Sun should be drawn and colored yellow in picture.

Page 62
1. Stop; 2. Go; 3. Stop; 4. Go; 5. Traffic signs keep you safe.

Page 63
1. Answers will vary but may include bikes, wagons, trucks, trains, cars, or planes.

Page 64
1. B; 2. C; 3. A; 4. Answers will vary but may include his egg head would have cracked.

Page 65
1. B; 2. A; 3. C

Answer Key

Page 67
1. Pollution makes the air unsafe to breathe. 2. Smoke, cars, and cutting down too many trees cause air pollution. 3. plant more trees; find a safer way to burn things; drive their cars less. 4. Drawings will vary but should reflect knowledge of solutions to pollution.

Page 68
1. rain; 2. hot; 3. dry; 4. to tell how hot and dry the desert is

Page 69
1. D; 2. C; 3. B; 4. A; 5. to tell about different kinds of trees

Page 70
1. D; 2. E; 3. C; 4. A; 5. B

Page 71
1. Pictures of boy sleeping and glass of water should be circled.

Page 72
1. C; 2. A; 3. C; 4. A

Page 73
1. B; 2. B; 3. C; 4. C

Pages 74–75
1. circled: dog running around town, girl in an airplane, boy at library, children in boat; 2. in order of occurrence: loves, likes, loves

Page 76
1. Sean is happy. His garden should look healthy with lots of plants growing. Robert is sad. His garden should look unhealthy with drooping plants. 2. Answers will vary. 3. Pictures will vary.

Page 77
1. B; 2. B; 3. C; 4. A

Page 78
1. B; 2. C; 3. B; 4. Answers will vary.

Page 79
1. No. Answers will vary but may include that the poem uses the word *if* and people do not have wings. 2. B; 3. Answers will vary.

Pages 80–81
1. No, Sentences will vary. 2. Yes; 3. Yes; 4. No, Sentences will vary. 5. Drawings will vary but should reflect understanding of distinction between reality and fantasy.

Page 82
1. A; 2. B; 3. B; 4. B

Page 83
1. F; 2. O; 3. F; 4. O; 5. F; 6. F; 7. to tell about the job of a firefighter

Page 84
1. D; 2. B; 3. Answers will vary but should include an opinion.

Page 85
1. O; 2. O; 3. F; 4. F; 5. F; 6. O; 7. Answers will vary but may include cries, crying, likes, or smile. 8. Answers will vary.

Answer Key

Page 86
1. F, O, O, F; 2. Answers will vary but should reflect knowledge of distinction between fact and opinion.

Page 87
1. A; 2. C; 3. B; 4. C

Page 88
1. B; 2. B; 3. C; 4. A and D should be circled. 5. Answers will vary but should include an opinion.

Page 89
1. C; 2. B; 3. A

Page 90
1. C; 2. D; 3. A; 4. B; 5. Riddles will vary.

Page 91
1. It was raining outside. 2. No, No, Yes, No

Page 92
1. C; 2. D; 3. A; 4. E; 5. B; 6. Ocean Land

Page 93
1. Anna's Height: tall, Anna's Hair Color: black; Anna's Sport: basketball, How Anna Feels: happy, proud

Page 95
1. sad dog; 2. Answers will vary but should reflect Barker feels sad. 3. happy dog; 4. Answers will vary but should reflect that Barker feels happy and needed. 5. Answers will vary but should reflect knowledge that Barker's feelings changed because Barker did something important, something that made her feel special.

Page 96
1. B; 2. A; 3. C; 4. B

Page 97
1. C; 2. A; 3. B; 4. B

Page 98
1. D; 2. C; 3. A; 4. B; 5. to tell about busy airports

Page 99
1. F; 2. T; 3. T; 4. T; 5. F; 6. F; 7. F; 8. wonderful

Pages 100–101
1. boy racing down stairs; 2. sunset on lake near forest; 3. submarine; 4. mountaintop; 5. Answers and drawings will vary.

Page 102
1. A; 2. D; 3. B; 4. C

Page 103
1. A; 2. C; 3. C; 4. A

Page 104
1. a turtle; 2. an owl; 3. polite; 4. Answers will vary but may include that a turtle's shell can look like a rock. 5. He went to sleep.

Page 105
1. C; 2. A; 3. A; 4. B

Page 106
1. B; 2. B; 3. C; 4. C

Page 107
1. C; 2. B; 3. C; 4. Answers will vary.

Answer Key

Page 108
1. B; 2. A; 3. C; 4. A

Page 109
1. Stage should show the following: starfish near table wearing purple scarf, crab at middle of stage wearing gold crown, sea horse near mirror wearing red bow, electric eel wrapped around pole, and dolphin beside the curtain. Check students' coloring.

Page 110
1. hoop; 2. Drawings will vary but should reflect understanding of position word *over*. 3. Drawings will vary but should reflect understanding of position word *under*. 4. Drawings will vary but should reflect understanding of position word *behind*.

Page 111
1–6. Picture should show a blue pond, gray elephant, purple short flowers, orange tall flowers, a green circle around the vegetable garden, and pencil marks indicating water coming from elephant's trunk and watering the gardens.

Page 112
wheels, round, people, down, town

Page 113
are, Up, sky, star, wonder

Page 114
down, crown, fiddle, moon, spoon; Drawings will vary.

Page 115
In order of occurrence: grows, grows, grain, grapes, green beans, grain

Page 116
1. Some; 2. All; 3. No; 4. Many; 5. Drawings will vary.

Page 117
1. Some; 2. All; 3. No; 4. Most; 5. to compare birds

Page 118
bird, ant, snake, tree frog, mammal

Page 119
1. jaguar and monkey; 2. snake; 3. ant; 4. Answers will vary but may include beetle or butterfly.

Page 121
1–4. Answers will vary.

Page 122
1. robin; 2. pelican; 3. seven; 4. New Hampshire